I KICKED THE DEVIL IN THE SHINS

MARK BYRNE

 A CIP catalogue record of this book is available from the British Library

Published by
On the edge Books
Goretti, Diamond Hill
Roundwood,
County Wicklow
Ireland

Cover Design
Slick Fish

Printed & bound in Ireland by
ColourBooks Ltd., Dublin

ISBN: 0 9538955 0 5

Contents

To Mam, Dad, Ruth & John.

To Marisa and all who have kicked the devil in the shins.

Foreword by Tom O'Riordan

The courage of those who have overcome the unexpected difficulties in life are sometimes as deserving of those precious medals of gold as those fortunate enough to win them in the sporting arena itself. Mark Byrne is one of those people, wholesome in spirit, unforgiving in his quest to hang on to that which is dearest to us all, life itself. Others before him have shown similar courage, like the incredible Fanahan McSweeney, but Mark's ability to battle against the odds and come out with a smile on his face is what makes this book so special.

Running in the black vest of Blackrock AC he was an athlete who resembled one of those flying Kiwi's that graced the Olympic arena. However he never got the chance to fulfil his dreams or true potential as one of the country's best 800 metre runners and yet his untimely illness ignited a fire of determination within which has given him that sense of fulfilment which he experienced and cherished during his University days in Tennessee, and Pocatello, Idaho.

In this book Mark is true to himself, his family and his friends and as he admitted in one chapter it was his strong mind and not wanting to fail which remained constant throughout his life.

On that August day in 1984 when he kissed his family goodbye at Dublin airport to cross the Atlantic to the USA to take up his athletic scholarship he could never have foreseen that eight years later he would be lying ill in at St

Bartholomew's Hospital in London and facing an uncertain future.

To have emerged from that nightmare with a new philosophy in life is what makes this book such a compelling read and also serves as an inspiration for those who might be inclined to think that sometimes there may not be light at the end of the tunnel. Mark Byrne is that light.

Acknowledgements

Writing an acknowledgement is an impossible task because so many people have been involved over the years that I cannot possibly name them all. However, I would like to take the opportunity to issue a general thanks to one and all who have helped be it by visits, encouragement, concern, kindness, prayers or friendship. I am eternally grateful. To all the wonderful nurses, doctors and staff at St Bartholomew's and the London Hospital for their numerous hours of dedication and skill. To all the GPs past and present.

I owe thanks to several people whose professional skills helped to bring this book to publication. To Paul Dolan and staff at Colourbooks for all the help and advice on printing, binding and book production, Slick Fish Design, to Tom O'Riordan, for advice, encouragement and help, to Siobhan Mullet, Anne Evans, John Harvey. To Frank Greally, The Irish Runner Magazine, John Treacy and Catherina McKiernan. A special thanks to Jonathan Williams for his many hours of advice, wit, knowledge and skill. To all at I.S.U, to Brian and Elizabeth, Dave, Glen, Pauline, to Brent, Gary and Roger, to all the lads at Blackrock club. To the staff, pupils and parents at St Mary's and St Edmund's, the Grant Family, the Dynan and Mc'Donnell families, Phil and Carmel, Eddie and Sadie, Dinah, Peter, Ciarán and Sandra, Tom and Mary, Barbara and Caroline, Phil and Bev, Alison and Murray, Simone, Steve and Mims, Cory and Mike, James, Anne, Aidan, James, Aidan, Dominic, Jane, Anne, Madeleine, Peter, Amadeo, Clara & Paula, to Michele for being a great friend and source of humour, to the lads, Pat, Paula, Tom, Jean, Christy, Bernie, Lar, Dympna, Dominic, Adrienne, Dermot, Catherine, Jamie, Wendy, Kevin, Maura, Steve, Dick, Gary. Especially to the McClary Family, Madge, Ian and Catherine who have looked after me since the beginning and have been true loving friends throughout. I called on Madge more times than I care to remember and she always dropped everything to come to my rescue. To Margarita for taking me in as a son and loving me like a mother. To Mam, Dad, Ruth, John, Dermot and Norah for being the most wonderful, supportive, loving family a person could wish for. I love you all and thank you for being there for me on so many occasions. Without your love and support I would not be here to write this book. Finally to Marisa who put up with me while I wrote this book but more importantly loved me at my weakest and looked after me at my most vulnerable under incredibly trying circumstances. Words cannot describe my gratitude. You are my every thing, my best friend. Blue skies up ahead. Muchas Gracias.

Mark Byrne May 2000

TRIBUTE TO MY FATHER

We've often mourned noted men of worth
Who silently passed from this planet earth,
But ne'er was one so lamented by us all,
Whose loss hangs over Dalkey like a pall,
As last 'Man of Nature', brave John Byrne
I knew him well for over thirty years,
A favourite with all his compeers;
His pleasing conversations unarmed his foes,
And his friends from him sought comfort in their woes
I talked with him on many a topic cramp,
And found his knowledge lively - never damp,
A bricklayer by trade he made his mark,
At plummet's law he ne'er was in the dark,
For many buildings testify this truth
From here to Dublin and far famed Maynooth.
His many bearing and good–natured face
For him made scores of friends in every place.
When health broke down he still remembered all
That happened since his youth both great and small
He loved his family with an ardent will,
Inherited his father's name and father's skill,
Farewell good John, though you rest in clay,
This tribute of respect to you I pay

Adapted from a poem by my Great-Grandfather
Michael Fanning (1840 –1923)

PART ONE

1

THE MAN WITH THE PLAN

I always wanted to run in the Olympics. Steve Ovett and Sebastian Coe were setting the world athletic scene on fire when I was a teenager and I wanted to be like them. But it went way back. Back to Herb Elliott and Zatopek and Snell. I also wanted to be a Physical Education teacher because I loved sport, all sport. I could teach P.E in the winter and run the 800 metres in the summer. It was that simple. That is what I wanted in life.

I had plan A. Grow up, become the best 800 metres runner in the world, win the Olympics and be a Physical Education teacher. Not a bad dream when you analyse it. Ireland had not won a Gold medal in an Olympic track event since Ronnie Delany in 1956 and if I won the 800 metres final then I would be a hero. I'd be a household name like Eamonn Coghlan, John Treacy, Barry McGuigan and Seán Kelly. I had it all worked out. I'd be in fourth or fifth coming off the last bend with a hundred metres to go in the final and then

I'd make my move, sprinting like the clappers past everyone. Bill O'Herlihy would be going mad on RTE, people jumping up and down in pubs all over the place, going wild celebrating on the streets of Dublin singing Olé Olé Olé. I'd do a lap of honour draped in the tricolour. Imagine the glory, the excitement. I'd get a great welcome home, the freedom of Dublin and guest appearances on The Late Late Show and Parkinson would surely follow. Everyone would know who Mark Byrne was.

The only problem with my plan was that there was no plan B. Later on in life Madge McClary would tell me that you always had to have a plan B. Some people even needed a C and a D plan because life can get that complicated. But at sixteen, plan A was good enough for me. That was how it stayed until I was 27 when I started running down the alphabet of plans. How did this happen? Well I'll try to explain by saying that I had a few defining moments. I suppose everybody has had defining moments. This is my story.

2

THE TERMINATORS

It is early in the morning and I have just opened my eyes. I was woken from my dreams by one of the 'Terminators', who at this hour of the morning sounds like Krakatau ready to explode. Although I have never seen a 'Terminator', I am grateful to them as they let me know that I am still alive. One day I fully expect Arnie to burst through the wall spitting bullets.

Right now I am physically and mentally very weak and living in room 9 of Bodley Scott Three in Saint Bartholomew's hospital in London. My girlfriend Marisa is with me, although I cannot actually see her because she is asleep on a mattress on the floor. We have been together ten months now, since October 1993. She is from Melilla, a province of Spain in North Africa. She is typical Spanish-looking; just five feet tall, tanned, long black hair, brown eyes and very pretty.

We have been through so much in our short relationship that if we survive this then there is great hope for us. This place has become our home and yet I do not want to be here even one day longer. I know that I am on the edge and barely hanging on. I am like a boxer who has been knocked down twice for a six count but is still on his feet hanging on until the bell can save him. Of course I was not always like this and, like Marlon Brando in 'On the Waterfront', I could have been a champion.

Bang! There goes another 'Terminator'. The 'Terminators' is a name that Marisa and I have for some people who come around the wards at six every morning collecting dirty linen and boxes from the supply rooms. They create so much noise with their trolleys and banging doors that I always hum Fleetwood Mac's song 'The Chain' and hear Murray Walker's voice describing the action for the Formula One races.

I endeavour to sit up. My bottom is killing me and 'ooh ah Cantona' has a new meaning when your coccyx, or man's vestigal tail hurts like hell. Old habits die hard and instinctively I take my pulse. I do it every morning and have done so since I first starting running seriously at about the age of twelve. My pulse is racing along and it is ninety-five just lying here. My resting heart rate used to be fifty. Despite that, I still dream of getting back to the track one day, putting on my spikes and running a really fast track session.

My mind is working hard to make sense of my life. You see I am trying to survive, to stay alive. I want to get out of this bed, this room, this hospital, because my innate will to live is still alive. Wanting to survive and believing in my dreams is the most vital weapon in my armoury. The pursuit of my dreams has led to substantial highs and lows in my life but I believe that in order to have life one must have dreams.

My dream now is to get better and to write a book about all that has happened. I want to write it not only to exorcise the nightmares but also to help others to cope with and to make sense of their own traumas and problems. I have known many for whom the struggle to survive has proved too great. Their faces are etched in my memory forever. Friends and comrades who shared a unique experience and whose courage, humour and dignity are an inspiration to me now as I strive to survive and write my story. But where to start?

I suppose the summer of 1992 was the turning point. I spent six weeks travelling alone around Europe and it was a major turning point in my life. I tasted alcohol for the first time and did not race on a running track for the first time since I was twelve. Amazingly I returned rejuvenated and ready for a new beginning. My life had lacked direction and I realised that I needed to leave teaching or else my running career was over. I wanted to go to Australia with Brent Caudill, a friend and athlete, and start training again. My letter of resignation had been accepted at the school and I could leave in December. All I had to do was survive teaching for a few months and I was gone. Just thinking about it made my heart pound. I knew we could stay with Roger Gall in Sydney and with a lot of hard work I could regain my fitness. The Olympic dream was back on.

One October night, while I was on boarding duty, my sister rang.

'Dad came through the operation okay but he is very sick. The doctors say it went well but that he might be very weak for a long time.'

I had known for a while that Dad was due to go into hospital for an operation, but had not known whether it was serious or not.

'It was a big operation and they discovered some lumps in his stomach which they removed.'

'Lumps,' I said. 'Cancer?'

'Yes. Please God they got it all out.'

'But sure Dad never smoked or drank in his life. He is very strong and fit. How could he get cancer?'

'Who knows? We are all in shock.' Despite my best efforts, my body started to shake and the tears came monsoon style.

'I'll come home,' I sobbed.

I took some days off work and flew home. My Dad had aged incredibly and I got a terrible fright when I went to see him in the hospital. He was weak, in a state of shock and seriously ill. They had removed three-quarters of my Dad's stomach and all the cancer that they could see, but there was no guarantee that it was all gone. At best he had three to six months; maybe less, maybe more. Nobody knew. All we could do was hope and pray.

His illness was a massive blow to the whole family. To see somebody who was so kind and full of life alter so dramatically was terrifying. My Dad was of a slight build, yet he was incredibly strong, and once he set his mind on something he usually achieved it. We had to pray that his iron will would help him defy the odds and get better.

I went back to England and rang Brent in America and Roger in Australia to tell them that I could not leave England. Dad's illness put the disappointment of not being able to travel into perspective. We all would gladly have traded anything for his health to be restored and I found it very hard to believe that he was so ill after having led such a healthy life.

Christmas arrived and, as the school had not hired anyone, I continued to work there. Naturally my running suffered but I kept training as it helped me to come to terms with Dad's illness and the job. Running helped focus my mind and restore normality to my life. It was a necessary drug I needed. For an hour or two I could lose myself in my training.

I went home for Christmas to stay with my parents and for a badly needed rest. There was no change with Dad. Sometimes there was a sparkle of his old self for a few minutes but then it would fade again. It was hard work for my Mum to see him so dejected, yet having him home again was brilliant. The whole family came together many times. This was made easy by the fact that my sister Ruth and her husband Dermot now lived in the same village with their children, Aisling, Tara, and Simon. My brother John lived on the south side of Dublin and came up to Wicklow regularly. It was a time for reflection for us all as we prayed for my Dad and hoped that the New Year would herald a new dawn.

Back at St Edmund's, in the first week of January 1993, I joined the majority of the staff in complaining that the Christmas holidays had passed too quickly. The break had failed to rid me of the fatigue that plagued me, and every day I seemed to have a pain in my stomach. It was with some surprise, however, that I woke up on the morning of 19 January 1993 to discover a lump the size of a golf ball on the left side of my neck. I immediately went to my doctor in Bishop's Stortford. He was a plump, friendly man who gave me a meticulous examination. I was incredibly calm as I assumed that it was a virus or a pulled muscle and that I'd need some vitamins and possibly a few days' rest.

'We need to take some X-rays as I am not happy with that gland. I'll sign you off work immediately.'

'Are you sure that is necessary?'

'You cannot afford to get hit with a ball on that lump and we'll need to look at your stomach as well. It is best to make sure we sort things out properly.'

I had no idea what was wrong and therefore I left the surgery feeling confident that I would get better shortly. Back at the school I helped Michele finish off a swimming gala and showed some of the staff my lump. It was quickly nicknamed 'The Alien'.

On arrival at the Herts and Essex Hospital in Bishop's Stortford, I was given a gown to change into. Minutes later I took my place on the bench beside half a dozen women waiting for Ultra-sound scans. Bump after bump greeted my eyes as I scanned down the line of expectant mothers. They were all staring at each other and me and I began to feel paranoid. Maybe they think I did that to all of them. A stern Sister approached me.

'Would you mind going back to the changing rooms? Your gown is on back to front and you are revealing yourself to these women.'

'Oh,' I answered a little flustered. 'Nothing they all haven't seen before by the looks of it,' and I toddled off.

Ruth and John came over for the weekend to lend support and took me to Harlow hospital for a test called a Bone Marrow sample. In a small confined room a short stocky doctor administered a local anaesthetic into my left hip. He reminded me of a nasty little gnome. He must have read my mind because he sure made me suffer.

It felt like a drill was going into me, deeper and deeper. He started to explain the process to a trainee who was also in the room. Obviously I could not see what was going on but the burning sensation increased with every passing second and I became ever more uncomfortable. Shut up talking I thought, or I'll puke all over you.

'How much longer? It feels like you're drilling for oil. Are you sure you used enough anaesthetic?'

'Just a little more.'

He resumed, explaining in detail what he was doing. My stomach churned once more. I hate this guy, I thought, and bit into my hand with the pain.

'That really hurts. I'll never complain about a dentist for as long as I live,' I whined, gritting my teeth in agony. I heard a bone snap and the doctor suddenly shout: 'There it is! Jackpot!'

'Ow, Jayzus that hurt,' I yelled.

Then, all hell broke out. I suddenly heard a loud groan followed by a thump as someone hit the floor. Cries for help rang out from the room as my marrow started to flow. I prayed that it was not the doctor collecting the samples who had fainted.

'What's happening?' I wailed.

'Don't worry. Everything's fine. I have the sample.'

'Thank the holy for that,' I said, perspiration dripping from my brow.

Help arrived and the fallen trainee was taken from the room. I was cleaned up and abandoned to walk down the corridor, feeling like I had been kicked by a Grand National winner. The pain was the most excruciating and unpleasant experience of my life; I never wanted to go through it again. The word revenge instantly sprang to mind.

'You're a great man,' said John. 'We're proud of you.'

'You are the best, Mark,' Ruth said and hugged me.

'I'm not really. It was bloody awful,' I said and burst out crying.

Even though I could not work, I still spent time with my friends and colleagues at work. Nobody could believe that anything serious was wrong with such a young, fit, lively person as myself. Many of the students and staff sent get well cards and letters of support to me. It was a frustrating time not being able to run or do any physical activity and all I could do was stretch and do light yoga exercises in my room.

The problem facing my family was that my father was still incredibly weak and trying to come to terms with his own illness. We wanted to know what was wrong with me first before saying anything, as we were afraid that the shock of more bad news might be too great for him.

Between 20 January and 12 February I underwent every examination, blood test, X-ray and scan available to the medical profession. It was a difficult time, culminating with the biopsy on 28 January 1993. I entered Princess Alexandra Hospital in Harlow the night before the biopsy and was shown to a bed. It was on a big mixed double ward with sixteen patients, mostly in their sixties and seventies. I delayed the inevitable, procrastinating for as long as possible until eventually I changed from my civvies into my pyjamas. A hospital band was put on my wrist, my transformation complete. It was obvious that now I was just another number.

A young doctor arrived and drew a massive circle around 'The Alien' with a thick blue marker pen. 'We have to identify the side for the operation.'

'You don't think they'll spot Sigourney's pal perched on my neck,' I replied sarcastically.

She gave me a tablet to help me relax but a few minutes later Simone and Alison arrived to wish me luck. They were my teaching colleagues at my former school, Saint Mary's, in Bishop's Stortford. They chatted away excitedly and even followed my bed down to the theatre.

On arrival I was deposited in a small room. My heart was racing along as if I was about to toe the line for a track race. My adrenal glands were working overtime as time slowed to a millisecond. Nothing moved and the beat of my heart filled the room like a bass guitar cranking out a tune. Then the door opened; resembling a scene from a B Horror movie, and a group approached, all dressed in green gowns, facemasks and gloves.

'I am the anaesthetist,' a voice whispered softly. 'Are you ready for a little nap?'

'Not too little. I would not want to suddenly spring to life at a vital moment and scare the hell out of everyone.' There was a chorus of laughter and then 'The Voice' took hold of my hand and I felt the sting of the needle as the icy cold drug entered my veins. My eyes started to close slowly and I was gone.

I came to to find John and Ruth sitting by my bed. My neck was heavily bandaged. The pain was dreadful and, as I attempted to move, it stung all the deeper.

'You have been back a couple of hours,' Ruth said, coming up beside me. 'How are you feeling?'

'Terrible. I don't think that I will ever straighten my neck again. Is there a huge hole there?'

'The surgeon said everything went well,' added John. 'It looks like a lad just took a bite out of you.' (A lad was a family slang name for anything, interchangeable with lots of words depending on the context of the sentence.)

I spent a frustrating and painful week in Harlow but eventually I was let out to convalesce in my friend Madge McClary's house. She worked and lived at St Edmund's and offered to look after me until my strength returned. John and Ruth came back over again. Ruth stayed with Phil and Bev Davies, while John stayed in Madge's house. They told Dad that I had a chest infection and I wanted them to visit for a while.

The next night I began to have problems breathing. I didn't wake anyone but walked around the room convincing myself that it was wind, and that it would go away. At six in the morning John found me on all fours desperately sucking for air. Madge immediately brought me back to the hospital; for the first time I realised that something serious was wrong with me.

At Harlow, terms like collapsed lung and pneumonia were forwarded as possibilities. I didn't care so long as I was given something for the terrible pain and something to help me breathe. A nurse stabbed me viciously in the thigh and I threw up all over her. My lungs felt as though someone had a voodoo doll of me and was using it for darts practice. They put me back on a double ward but because of my distress and the noise of all the machines there, I was moved into the television room for peace. Unfortunately, a few hours later, a nurse woke me up to give me a sleeping tablet, after which I could not get back to sleep.

After three slow boring days a small thin doctor arrived at my bedside.

'We are going to transfer you to a hospital in London for further examinations,' he informed me suddenly.

'Is it that serious?'

'Don't be alarmed. Be happy that you are going to a hospital with an excellent reputation. They will conduct some more tests and give you all the results in London. I have great confidence in them.'

I kept the curtains closed after he left because I wanted some privacy. Cocooned from the rest of the ward, I mulled over what he had told me. At first I was worried about the sudden change but after hours of deliberation I convinced myself that it did not matter where I went, even if I had to go back to America, so long as I received the best possible help and expertise available. I took out my diary and wrote down all my thoughts. I had always kept a diary to record my training and race results and it was also a good way of expressing my thoughts and feelings. I sometimes felt that once I wrote things down I understood them better. It was similar to going out for a run in that it helped me to see things clearer. So that night, since I could not run, I wrote.

3

BORN TO RUN

'You're on your bike, Mark. Go on, kick harder, harder.'

My Dad was sprinting along the grassy verge with my coach Dermot as I headed towards the finish line of the under thirteens' cross-country championships. My head was shaking badly, my nails dug into my hands as I clenched my fists and pumped my knees like pistons. Inch by inch I could feel myself getting ahead of my nearest rival, his arms behind mine, his breathing heavier, struggling. Then, with fifty yards to go, he snapped and I sprinted for the line, collapsing into my father's arms, barely able to breathe.

'You're all right, son. You won! You won!'

I was born in 1964. My memories of being brought up in Blackrock, seven miles from Dublin, are very pleasant ones. My Dad was a bricklayer by trade who built his own house in his home village of Dalkey. Soon after my parents married, the building trade was hit badly; they were forced to sell up and emigrate to America. My sister Ruth, who was one and a half at the time and had long curly red hair, was a big hit with the people in San Antonio, Texas. There my parents eventually settled close to two of my Dad's sisters, Geraldine and Gerty.

Three years later the economy in Ireland picked up and Mam and Dad returned because they were expecting another arrival, my brother John. Later Dad was promoted to Housing Inspector for Dun Laoghaire Corporation which took him away from his tools and the hard labouring on the building sites. Mam did various part-time jobs while also caring for three children. My parents worked incredibly hard and eventually saved enough money to buy their house from the corporation and then move to a bigger one.

The school's motto at Christian Brothers College in Monkstown is 'certa bonum certamen' which means, 'fight the good fight'. By the time I entered the secondary school there, John was seventeen and studying for the Leaving Certificate. Ruth had qualified as a hairdresser. There was not enough time in the day for me as I rushed in from school, wolfed down some food, and headed off to run, to play rugby, or to play football on the streets. No matter what sport I came in contact with, I savoured, but I realised that I was best at running and enjoyed it more than anything. I loved the freedom and power I felt when out on a run and the fact that no teammates, machines, or animals could affect my performance.

When I was twelve I joined Monkstown Running Club. Dermot Butler was the coach and he took me out with him three times a week to a long winding hill called Willie Gambles Hill in Monkstown. He drove beside me shouting out times and instructions as I ran up it. Once I got to the top, he would drive me back down to start again. Dermot moved away to marry and the club broke up, so I joined Blackrock Club where my neighbours Pat, Tom, and Christy Kenny were members. I went there three times a week to train on a hilly grass track. The rest of the time I trained alone. I knew I had the potential to do well but that if I wanted to become world-class then I had to get a scholarship to America where I could study for a degree and where the facilities and competition were far superior to those at home. This became my main ambition in life.

In July 1982 I turned eighteen and finished school. I went to a college in Dublin but soon dropped out, drifting into various government schemes which paid me some money and allowed me time to train. My parents were fantastic in their support and backed me all the way. The outdoor track season lasted from late April to August, during which months I raced to achieve the times necessary to get to America. Nineteen eighty-three came and went but I did not get any offers. I feared that I was living in dreamland and that I would end up like an aspiring Hollywood actor, auditioning every day, hoping for a break but never making it.

My life revolved around my running. I devoted all my energy into trying to improve. On Sunday afternoons my parents helped me to collect seaweed for baths to help my muscles. I went to yoga classes, took desiccated liver, cod liver oil and vitamin tablets and trained harder than ever. I watched videos and studied the training schedules of athletes like Herb Elliott and Peter Snell. Ian Hamilton arrived at Blackrock and I learned a lot from him as he had run for Villanova in Pennsylvania in the sixties. Dad hung a punch bag in the garage for me and I moved all my weights in there. Several of us from the club began swimming in the Forty Foot in Sandycove to help our muscles recover from the training.

My Leaving Certificate results were good enough and the American universities were interested in how fast I could run the 400, 800 and 1500 metres. Throughout the winter I ran about sixty miles a week with weight training and cycling as extras. As the summer approached I switched to the track sessions, where a typical workout would be either 5 x 400 metres with an two lap recovery or as the races drew closer 6 x 200 metres with a lap jog recovery. At night I always stretched in my room for a least forty minutes and took hot baths whenever I could to help my sore muscles.

The track season arrived and immediately my times improved. I was stronger and full of confidence and with the lads from Blackrock I travelled the country racing at all three distances. I improved sufficiently to be offered a place at Middle Tennessee University where Dean Hayes had been the Track Coach for twenty-one years. He was very experienced and had coached the USA jumps events in the World

Student Games and the 1976 and 1980 Olympics. The university was in the town of Murfreesboro, about thirty miles south of Nashville.

At Dublin Airport on 11 August 1984 I was surrounded by my family and a dozen friends. At last I was going to America. This was my dream come true and I was determined to make the most of my opportunity. Images of the Irish flag, Olympic glory and world fame flashed through my mind as I touched down in Tennessee. As soon as I walked out of the terminal at Nashville, the incredible heat and humidity almost knocked me off my feet. Instantly I realised what a challenge the climate would pose to my running.

'Welcome to the land of Elvis, Country and Western, and of course Jack Daniels,' Coach Hayes said in a deep southern drawl. 'I hope that you only sample that particular pleasure on rare occasions.'

'Who is Jack Daniels?'

'What? An Irishman who doesn't know that! It's Tennessee whisky, of course.'

'That explains it. I'm a pioneer.'

'A pioneer! Like them pilgrims in the north?'

'No. I don't drink; never have.'

'Irish,' he proclaimed laughing, 'you certainly are different and, with hair like that, you're going to be a big hit.'

Later that day he showed me around the university's campus and then presented me to the track team of forty athletes. There were only six white people in the room and I soon became the focus of attention. I was the first foreigner many of them had ever met and my shoulder-length hair and pale freckled skin fascinated them.

'Hey man, you sure has the reddest hair I ever seen,' followed by, 'Boy have you been hiding in the shade? Get yourself a tan.' 'Your mama must a covered you with protection forty cream cause you is the whitest man on earth,' and 'Red, when all them freckles join up, you'll have one hell of a tan.'

It took me a long time to settle into my new surroundings as I tried to cope with the strenuous training, heat, humidity, food, and the southern drawl. Soon I was known by 'Crazy old Red', 'Ronald McDonald' or 'The Olympic Torch'. All the athletes followed the same routine of breakfast at seven, classes until midday, lunch and then off to training at three o' clock. The evening was for study, or in my case recovery. I shared a room with a black guy from Tennessee called Jerry. We had a bed, a desk, and a wardrobe each. The three toilets, wash basins and showers were for everyone in our block. Everything was open plan; no doors on anything! It was some experience trying to hold a conversation with someone while suffering diarrhoea, with no door to hide behind to conceal one's embarrassment and discomfort.

The weather in Tennessee was hot and humid for most of the year. The cross-country season was from September to December and a squad of about thirteen athletes travelled around the south racing each weekend in order to pick a team of six for the Conference finals. Cross country in Ireland was over wet, muddy, fields in cold damp conditions but in Tennessee it was five miles on a flat golf course in seventy degree heat. Even at home I had always struggled in cross-country races and used them purely as strength-building sessions for the track season. In my first term I found it very tough and struggled into the team at number six.

All the major universities in America competed against each other in different Conferences. Our Conference included universities from Tennessee, Ohio, Georgia and Alabama and to win the conference final as an individual or a team was the main goal of the season. I performed poorly at the finals and was conscious of the fact that some members of the team seemed pleased at my failure.

One day I went to talk to Coach Hayes and told him how worried I was about my running and my studies.

'Red, you are doing fine,' he said. 'It is your first year here and as far as I am concerned your classes are going very well and you are dedicated to your running. You are used to just two seasons in Ireland; cross-country in the winter and track in the summer. Here it is competitive all year round and every kid on the track team wants more scholarship money because they believe that they are worth it. There are only twelve scholarships and sixty people trying out for the team. They know you are a foreigner and on a scholarship and so are keen to beat you. It will take you all this year to adjust. But I know that you have the potential, so if you can score even one single point in either the indoor or outdoor season then I will be a happy man.'

I felt a lot happier after talking to Coach Hayes. My belief in myself was restored and I vowed not to let him down.

Racing on the track in January and February was another completely new experience for me. The indoor track in Tennessee was a 280 yard flat track and it took me several track sessions to get used to the short tight bends. Tactically you had to be aware of your position, especially on the tight corners in order to either make a move or cover someone trying to get away. One mistake and it was almost impossible to recover from it. I used a lot of Vaseline on my feet because the sharp bends gave me blisters. I really enjoyed racing indoors and soon felt that I was now proving my worth to the team.

In the conference championships I easily qualified for the 800 metres final and the next day I finished fourth, scoring valuable points. We won the team title and, spurred on by my success, I began training for the outdoor season. The weather was extremely hot by May and it really bothered me, but in the outdoor Conference finals in Ohio I finished third in the 800 metres and fifth in the 1500 metres finals which encouraged me enormously. We completed the double by winning the team outdoor title, for which we received engraved rings as recognition of the achievement. As I headed home to Ireland for the summer, I was proud to have survived what is generally regarded as the toughest year of a scholarship. I set myself a goal of winning an individual title on my return.

Back home the lure of country living was growing stronger for my parents and, that summer, while I was training to regain my fitness, they realised a dream. On my twenty-first birthday they bought a little cottage in Roundwood, County Wicklow, the highest village in Ireland. The cottage was in need of total renovation, but they could see its potential. They transformed the place over the next ten years, and I would challenge anyone to find a more beautiful, tranquil, and scenic place.

The second year I moved into a house with Billy, Bob and Win, which we named 'The Time Pit'. Socially it was a great change for me because my American friends were rich and had the latest of everything. Life was good until a knee injury forced me to have an orthoscopic operation on it. This, on its own, was not too bad, but the university decided to drop Track from its programme and the entire track team had to find new universities to compete for. My knee operation actually worked to my advantage. Because I had not raced either indoors or outdoors in my second year at Tennessee I still had three years of competing left. I could now stay and race in my fifth year at university when I would be older and stronger. Eventually I secured an offer to go out west to Pocatello, Idaho.

In August 1986, still unfit from the operation, I flew to Pocatello via New York and Salt Lake City. Five thousand feet up in the Rocky Mountains, surrounded by excellent mountain trails, with a magnificent indoor stadium, a banked running track and weather that suited me better, Pocatello was a great move.

Dave Nielsen was the Head Coach, but it was under the watchful eye of Brian Janssen that my training altered. It now included three hard fast sessions a week on the track, combined with light, easy runs on the trails for recovery. We also went swimming at seven every morning as part of strength building and recovery sessions for sore muscles. Running from side to side in the shallow part and various exercises in the deep end helped maintain fitness but without the pounding effect on bones and joints.

I was strong-minded and did not want to fail, a characteristic that remained constant throughout my life. I pushed myself on the hard days but made sure I now listened to my body and took the time to recover properly on the rest days. It seems so obvious now but athletes can get caught up on running hard every day and running to the stopwatch instead of enjoying the training and becoming less obsessive and more professional. The coaches helped me to take in the whole picture and I learned to train for races and run fast times rather than to train blindly and leave it all on the training session.

The change worked and I was part of a two-mile relay team that ran 7 minutes 22 seconds indoors for two miles and went on to the America Championships in Oklahoma City. This was my first taste of success and it left me wanting more. My first year ended with full A's in my studies and my outdoor 800 metres time improved by three seconds to 1.50.3 when I came second in the championship final.

The 1987-88 season proved to be a real milestone. In August 1987 just two weeks after my twenty-third birthday, I married an Irish girl from Dublin.

We had been going out with each other for a few weeks before I left for America in 1984. She moved over to the States for my second year in Tennessee and then to Idaho. Life was good and it was reflected in my running.

Under Brian's coaching and the competition for places, my running continued to improve as I grew stronger and faster. I had a set routine and diet. My training went really well and I was experiencing new levels of fitness and confidence. In February I won my first 800 metres indoor Big Sky Conference title in 1.50.35 and qualified for the American Championships again. I was delighted not only with the time but also the fact that I was now strong enough to run four races in two days. That weekend I had run the heats and final of the 800 metres and the 4 x 800 relay and 4 x 400 relay.

I went into the outdoor season unbeaten over 800 metres and full of new belief in my ability to run fast times. The Seoul Olympics were going to take place that August and I secretly harboured thoughts of running a fast time close to qualifying standard. My training now involved carefully worked out sessions with Brian and Dave, which really improved my speed and strength. The plyometric drills and fast accelerating workout paid dividends, and with confidence sky high, I easily qualified for the Big Sky 800 metres Conference final in Moscow, Idaho.

The final started at a fast pace which was exactly what I wanted. I tucked in behind the leaders and tracked them down the back straight. I was concentrating hard and oblivious to anything outside the track. Up the home straight and the bell rattled loudly. I was lying third in 52 seconds. Down the back straight I moved into second, biding my time. Then off the last bend I kicked hard up the home straight into the lead. Crossing the line I was ecstatic to not only win but to see the clock flash 1.48.63. It was my best time by two seconds. It broke the stadium and the Idaho State University record.

4

A SLIPPERY SLOPE

I arrived home from America in July and within days a dream came true. The letter read:

03-06-88

Dear Mark,

I wish to inform you that you have been selected to compete for Ireland in Westathletic (Brussels) on 18/19 June 88.....

I stood on the track nervous and excited and soaked up the atmosphere. Adrenaline coursed through my body. I was about to accomplish a lifetime's ambition. The Heysel Stadium in Belgium was indeed a famous place to make my grand entrance onto the international scene for Ireland. My brother John was in the stands to witness my glorious debut.

Bang! The race started and I was caught sleeping. I sprinted after them like a startled rabbit and after the first one hundred metres we broke from our lanes and came together on the back straight. Suddenly they all slowed and I found myself in the lead. In the lead with only one hundred and fifty metres gone! Oh God help me!

Round the bend we went in a close group. Everybody was bunching up with the slow pace and there was a lot of elbowing and pushing. Up the home straight I led but I could feel the pursuing pack breathing down my neck. The bell rattled loudly at 56 seconds. Runners started to move up alongside me but I felt fine and accelerated because I did not want to get boxed in. Down the back straight and round the last bend I sped, in control and ready to sprint to fame and victory. What will the papers say? What will the kids at school think?

And then it happened! The Bear jumped on my back. I started to tighten up and go backwards as one by one the others raced passed me. My legs felt like lead, my breathing was heavy and my chest hurt. Every sinew, fibre and muscle seized up. I barely made it to the finish. Crashing over the line, I lay on the track heaving and coughing. I knew I had run a bad race by leading the whole way, setting myself up like that, showing everyone how inexperienced I was. What a disaster! LAST! Eighth out of eight! Suddenly a hand tapped me on the back and I turned around to see a track official standing there.

'You have been chosen for a drug test. This way please.'

'But I came last! Is it to show that drugs do not work?'

He led me off to the toilets where another official handed me two bottles and pointed to the urinals.

'Please fill both bottles. We have to observe you at all times to ensure the test is valid.'

After the excitement and the sheer exhaustion

of the race, I could not go. The minutes ticked slowly by and still no trickle. Finally after thirty minutes and litres of water I succeeded. The two samples were put into separate vials and sealed with wax and the Belgium stamp. I then signed a form and departed, dejected and very despondent. I went for a warm down and ran for about three miles to get the lactic acid and frustration out of my system. My performance on the track had been poor but I hoped the experience would help me and that I would do better the next time. That is, of course, if I ever got picked again!

After my first international in Belgium I was invited to run in a televised international in Belfast against, among others, the English star, Peter Elliott. I knew that I would run better after my experiences in Belgium and I felt everything was moving in the right direction until, four days before the race, a hatchet I was chopping wood with glanced off and stuck in my weak knee. Ruth's husband Dermot rushed me to the hospital and I received several stitches in my knee.

To make matters worse, the next week I received a letter to compete in Scotland in my second international for Ireland. Naturally I was very disappointed to miss the opportunity to compete in two big races and end my season so abruptly, yet it only increased my desire to get back into training and achieve bigger and better things in the future.

In August 1988 I began my last year at university full of confidence. Luckily, despite the big lump on my knee I was able to resume training. I trained hard to regain my fitness and the altitude and the fabulous indoor track helped enormously. I missed most of the indoor season with bronchitis but I still defended my indoors 800-metres title. By the outdoor season of 1989 I was back to my best and winning regularly. In the Big Sky final I ran 1.48.71 to win the outdoor title for a second time. This resulted in my being voted Athlete of the Championship by all the coaches.

The day I received my Honours Teaching degree in Physical Education and History, I realised that my five years in America had been an enormous success. In total I had won five Conference titles, raced in the American Championships twice, set two University records and had twice been voted Most Valuable Athlete. Many of my dreams had come true and I looked forward to the future with real hope.

During the summer I competed in the Irish National Championship in Cork and easily qualified for the final. Marcus O'Sullivan and Frank O'Mara, important names in Irish athletics because both were Indoor World Champions, did not have to run in the heats because they had raced in Europe earlier that week. It annoyed me that they received specialist treatment because the National Championships should be the same for everyone just as with the American system. Anything can happen in the qualifying rounds such as being tripped, spiked or just not qualifying because of a poor run. I had run the fastest 800 metres the previous year and the fastest or next fastest to date this year.

I ran a bad tactical race in the final and came second to Marcus O'Sullivan. Although I had not had the opportunity to race much since coming home from the States in May, I was furious at coming second and not making my mark on the Irish scene. A few weeks later I was picked for Ireland, coming third in a race in Scotland where I met one of my heroes, Steve Ovett. I ended 1989 ranked second fastest in Ireland for the 800 metres.

My biggest disappointment on arriving back home was that the Department of Education dragged their feet in recognising my degree. Unemployment loomed. We needed the money and job security and when I was offered a job as a Physical Education and History Teacher at Saint Mary's in Bishop's Stortford, Hertfordshire, we moved to England. We were not getting on well. I worked during the day and trained at night. She got a job that involved shift work and we saw less of each other and started to grow apart.

My enthusiasm and commitment to running never deserted me, but the difference between being in America and England was huge. In the States I was a student enjoying fantastic support, great facilities, and top class expertise. In England I was a full-time teacher, struggling to find the time and energy to train and to keep a relationship going.

I joined the nearest big running club, Haringey, in north London. They competed in Division One, had a good track and several English international athletes. Work commitments limited my attendance there so I trained alone as best I could. My winter preparation was nothing like it had been in America but I went into the new season hopeful that I could still compete at the top level.

The 1990 season arrived and I ran the 800 metres in the British League for Haringey. To my surprise, I received another international call to go to Iceland to compete for Ireland. The headmaster of St Mary's, Robin Gregory, kindly allowed me to go at short notice. Halfway to Heathrow I realised that I had forgotten my passport but it was too late to go back. Luckily I was allowed into Iceland and back into England without any problems.

The race was slow throughout. There was a very strong wind blowing against the runners when we came into the home straight. With fifty metres to go I emerged from a tight bunch to win the race in a poor time. I did not care about the time. It was my first international win and I was naturally delighted. Later I marched out proudly to stand on the podium and receive my medal. Hearing the Irish National Anthem being played was indeed a sublime moment.

That night, at the athletes' dinner, I got terrible cramps in my hamstrings and was carried off by four people to be deposited in the ladies' toilets. The team physiotherapist was a woman and it was the only place where she could massage and help me. While I was lying on the floor pants down and the physiotherapist massaging my hamstrings, a very large Icelandic shot putter entered. She looked at us, went out again, checked that she was in the ladies, and then re-entered laughing.

Unfortunately my victory in Iceland was a rare high point. I had the opportunity to redeem my season at the National Championships in July but the reality of how much I had regressed since leaving America was brought home to me when I came third in a slow race. Despite receiving help and encouragement from Jamie and Sue Bevan, whom I had met through Haringey Club, my running continued to deteriorate. Instead of progressing from 1.48, I was now running three seconds slower.

It was not just that I was losing races and running poorly but that it felt so difficult. It was as if I was trying to ride a bike with the brakes on. The same old confidence and mental strength no longer existed and consequently I continued to produce appalling performances on a regular basis. Ever since arriving in England, I had struggled to come to terms with the loss of the facilities, the coaching and the life of a full-time athlete and my marriage problems.

My ambition had always been to run in the Olympics and the kind of progress I had made in America had encouraged me to that goal. Now, however, my dream was rapidly fading and with it all that I had trained so hard for. In a last ditch effort to save everything, I left St Mary's, a school I loved working at, so we could work on our relationship and I could return to full-time training. Despite regular training sessions with Jamie and Sue, I struggled to regain my fitness. I decided to go back to Idaho to get a break from all the emotional turmoil and to train with my coach, Brian, and the other runners there. On my return I competed in several big races where I had the opportunity to run fast times, but inexplicably, the season deteriorated. I could not block out the mental problems and all the negative vibes.

When I had dreamed of being an international star, I had really believed that I would make it, but now the doubts were flooding in. I desperately wanted to experience the old adrenaline rush as I stood on the line for the start of a race. I wanted to feel the power deep inside, the exhilaration and freedom of each stride as I kicked off the bend, accelerating with grace and invincibility.

Now my life was a mess. Everything suffered no matter what I did. The future was foreboding and grim; I felt that I was fooling myself to think I could re-invent my running career. The reality of not winning a major title or running in the Olympics rested heavily on my shoulders. It was the lowest point of my life; and a massive blow to all that I believed in and dreamed of.

I trained as hard as possible but the demands of teaching full-time and the stress in my life debilitated me both physically and mentally. Finally we separated permanently. There were no gory details to go into, just a relationship that left two people growing apart rather than together. It was no ones fault, just a sad demise into a fruitless relationship. Eventually it ended and we parted.

The same week that I planned to go back to Ireland to talk to Mam and Dad about everything, I applied for a teaching job at Saint Edmund's College, which was close to Bishop's Stortford. I was offered the post to start in January 1992 and immediately accepted since it not only offered money but also food, accommodation and a new start. I hoped that it would allow me time to decide what I wanted to do with my life. A few weeks later I fulfilled a childhood dream and went to see Arsenal play at Highbury.

Diary: 20 May 1992. My rooms at St Edmund's College.

As I lie on my bed listening to some music I feel like crying. I have been here five months now and I realise that my life has been blown totally off course. Where did it all go wrong? This new job is depressing me and sapping all of my energy. I am so unhappy, tired, and the combination of teaching and boarding duties is preventing me doing any proper training.

In the past I had structure, organisation and plenty of goals and ambitions. I was happy living the life of a professional athlete. Call it 'Runners High' or whatever, but feeling the power in my body as I ran, almost floating over the ground, freed my spirit in a special way. Some people find that release in drugs and alcohol, but for me it was running. It was all I ever wanted to do. Now I fear that all the years of training and sacrifice, everything I worked so hard for, is fading fast. Teaching is so demanding that it is impossible to train full time and I just cannot do two jobs at the same time. By the time five o' clock comes I am a spent force. My running is no longer the number one priority in my life and that is why I am unhappy. I hate living and working in the same place.

Last week I went to the doctor with sores on my face and he said it could be stress. Stress at my age, it's ridiculous and I am so stupid to have allowed this to happen. All that I cherish has vanished and I am now totally disillusioned. I am a shell of what I used to be. After all, like any good athlete, I know the signals from my body better than anyone else does and I have stopped listening to it. Anyone who competes in sport knows that defeat hurts. It is when it stops hurting and becomes the norm that it is time to stop. I have lost the hunger, the passion. I must act. My life is screaming out for change.

5

JUDGEMENT DAY

On 8 February 1993, I was transferred to Bodley Scott Three on the third floor of East wing at St Bartholomew's Hospital, London. As soon as I arrived on the ward, I was very relieved and impressed with its modern and comfortable surroundings. At the time of my transfer to Barts, I had no idea how good it was; all I hoped was that the people in it would be able to help me to get better. A tall, athletic young doctor arrived to talk to me.

'I am pleased to meet you, Mark. My name is Peter Johnson and I will be keeping an eye on you over the coming week as we conduct our own tests on the ward. If you are worried about anything, please let me know so we can talk about it.'

I liked Peter's pleasant manner and instantly felt secure and confident with him. Once again, John and Ruth came over and their support and encouragement was a huge boost. The tests consisted of more X-rays; scans and another bone marrow test and Peter drained fluid from my lung to help me breath more easily.

Because I had arrived from another hospital, I

was isolated in a side room until some swab results were analysed to see if I was carrying any contagious infections. I watched an indoor athletics meeting on the television and while it saddened me to see what I was missing, it also inspired me to get over whatever it was as quickly as possible so that I could get back to running again. The hospital routine continued on around me and I felt lonely. I agreed to allow a group of medical students examine me as I felt an affinity with them. Like me, they were just starting out on their journey of discovery. By the end of the week I was exhausted from it all. Peter came to talk to me.

'We have all the results and Professor Lister will see you tomorrow at ten o' clock to explain everything.'

Despite taking some sleeping tablets I could not sleep. Instead, I spent the night talking to myself like a boxer preparing for the big fight. I did not want to speculate about the future but preferred to be mentally prepared for whatever it was that fate had in store for me. It was imperative that I believed I could cope with anything.

The 12 February 1993 arrived. Judgement day! Ruth, John and I entered the room and were greeted by Elaine, the ward sister, Peter Johnson, and Professor Lister. Professor Lister headed the team of doctors and nurses on the oncology side at Barts. He was medium height, thin, wore a suit and dickey bow. Peter said that he was a highly respected authority on lymphomas and that I was in good hands.

Over the next hour the doctors covered lots of

information and details specifically relating to my cancer. We emerged from the meeting each of us lost in our own thoughts. It was hard to grasp everything. I knew that it would take several sessions before I really understood what was happening. I think that John and Ruth had feared the worst and were visibly relieved that at least treatment was available and that there was some light at the end of the tunnel.

I found out that I had Non-Hodgkin's Low-Grade B-Cell lymphoma. This is cancer of the Lymphatic System. There are two main types of Lymphoma, Hodgkin's Disease and Non-Hodgkin's. All cells repair and reproduce themselves in the same way but with Non-Hodgkin's Lymphoma which, like other cancers, is a disease of the body's cells, the process has got out of control. The cells continued to divide and developed into a lump or a tumour. My illness was specifically B-cell and low grade or slow-growing. The lymphatic system is part of the body's natural defence against infection and consists of nodes and glands all around the body joined by tiny lymphatic vessels. A clear fluid called lymph flows around the body and helps protect it against infection. The lymph fluid is drained via the lymphatics into the bloodstream. There are several major lymph nodes in the body at the groin, armpits, neck, chest and stomach, and these sieve through the lymph and attack the invaders.

I had problems in two of these areas: my neck, where the lump was removed, and my stomach. My stomach was the main concern as the tumours measured four and a half inches and this was the reason it was so hard and had hurt me recently. Given the extent of the spread and the nature of the disease, which had a tendency to recur, they told me that I would definitely need some form of chemotherapy. It then depended on how I responded to the treatment and what progress was made in stopping the cancer from spreading. Because I was very young for this type of cancer, the normal age bracket was fifty-five to sixty-five, they recommended that I start the treatment sooner rather than later.

I was shocked and disappointed. Nobody could explain why I was sick. I was twenty-eight, very fit, a non-smoker and had only tasted alcohol for the first time a few months ago. However, now that I had at last found out about the cancer, I wanted to concentrate on the future and get on with curing my illness. It was a matter of getting the chemotherapy and then waiting to see how successful it was and how much it affected my running and my job.

John and Ruth went to get lunch while I met with Peter to discuss the treatment. He told me that the chemotherapy drug was called chlorambucil. It would be in tablet form and he would work out a timetable later. He also said that they were conducting a study with a drug called Interferon. It was in a trial period and that they needed patients to volunteer for the project. They believed that it might be beneficial in treating cancer but needed to prove it through a five-year period. The study would then compare the results between those people who were treated with chemotherapy versus those treated with chemotherapy and Interferon. I agreed to be part of the study and waited for a computer to select at random which type of treatment to use. I knew that it would be helping cancer research and how people might be treated in the future.

The last thing we discussed was my sperm. Peter told me that the chemotherapy would damage it and that I might not be able to have children in the future. He advised me to store some before I started any chemotherapy in order to keep my options open. I went off for a walk to gather my thoughts and an hour later met up with Ruth and John in the square. We all hugged and went back to see Peter.

'You have drawn the combination of Interferon and chemotherapy,' he said. 'We will start treatment on 22 February to allow you to sort out things with your work and to go home and spend time with your family. It is very important to remain strong and have confidence in us.'

Going home was emotionally a very difficult time for me because of the precarious situation with my father. We decided to wait and see how I got on with the chemotherapy and the next set of results before saying anything to Dad. It was an incredibly difficult situation for everyone as he was still weak, withdrawn and subdued by the shock of his own condition and he would have been devastated if he had known that anyone else in the family also had cancer.

Mam was thrilled to see me and desperate to talk about everything, but it was not possible with my Dad in the house. He was a shrewd man and his brain was razor sharp. There were times when I really wanted to talk to him about everything but I fought against my desire. The excuse that I pulled a muscle in my neck to disguise the scar and my weakness from the operation helped. However, I knew that he thought it was strange that I was not running every day or even doing my indoor exercises and stretching, as had been my ritual since childhood.

I went out and bought some books about cancer and chemotherapy. It was important that I knew as much as possible about my illness as I felt it was to my advantage to be as knowledgeable as possible in dealing with it.

The last significant thing I did while at home was to inform all my close friends of the situation. The lads found it incredibly hard to take and they all came up to Roundwood for a drink and to talk about the bombshell I had dropped on them. We took over one of the pubs there; it was great to see them. Once the drinks were ordered and the table laden with pints, we start to discuss my news.

'It's all terribly sudden,' began Larry. 'Sure you were always the fittest.'

'What about the running?' asked Tom.

'Yeah, do you remember him when we played football,' interjected Pat, 'he never gave the ball to anyone but kept running until we got tired.' There was a chorus of agreement and then a sombre silence.

'So will you be out of a job?' asked Jamie.

'I don't know. I think I am entitled to some sick days but I have to sort it out with the school when I go back.'

'Where will you stay?' quizzed Dermot, 'and

what will you do for food?'

'Typical McCarthy,' joked Glougher, 'always thinking of his stomach. Feed me, Feed me,' he said, rubbing his own.

'I suppose no alcohol for you,' added Jamie with a look of injustice written all over his face.

'Well Doyler,' said Domo, 'you'd never survive without it that's for sure.'

There was a chorus of laughter and the night progressed onwards and upwards. Later, as I looked around the room at my friends joking and talking, I could almost taste the fear and shock they felt. It could have been any of them, the same age and background, and it scared them. They were deeply concerned, yet I knew that they all felt confident that I, their friend, who had suddenly at twenty-eight been struck with cancer, would make it. The evening made me realise that I was very lucky to have so many people to turn to for support and encouragement and they let me know with one voice that if anyone could make it, I could.

Despite spending some melancholy days staring out at the lakes, reflecting on the enormous changes that had occurred in the past few months, I returned to England feeling prepared for the fight that lay ahead. At home I received great support and encouragement from my family and friends. I now felt confident that I could deal with the chemotherapy and overcome the illness.

I entered the building somewhat nervously. It was an older, run down part of the hospital. I climbed the stairs praying that I would find a fellow male. Entering the laboratory, I was confronted by two woman in their fifties. Initially they ignored me and kept on talking. Then they stopped.

'Can I help you?' one of them asked?

'I have this,' I said handing them a paper from Peter.

'Oh,' came the reply as they looked at each other.

'Take two test tubes and fill them; I mean, and put a sample in them,' one said cheekily.

'The toilet is through there,' the other said pointing to the back of the lab. 'No rush.'

I grabbed the test tubes and headed for the toilet. It was a tiny, damp place. The window was broken and it had no toilet paper or towel. I burst out laughing. I went back to the two women, still talking. Before they could say a word I turned on them.

'Disgusting! Not even Picasso could find inspiration in there. I wouldn't ask two dogs to shag in it. Good-bye.'

A week later I went to a clinic in Harley street and performed my task. I did not have too many days left before the start of the chemotherapy and, having thought about Peter's advice, I felt he was right. I knew that by looking to the future I was taking the positive rather than the negative approach. After all I was living proof that life was full of twists and turns and I did not want to be in a position where I would regret not having acted. It might be the best choice I ever made, I told myself.

6

A REAL DILEMMA

I was in the grounds of St Bartholomew's when an old man befriended me.

'St Bartholomew's was founded in 1123 and is the oldest hospital in England,' he told me. 'Are you a patient or a visitor?'

'A patient. First day actually.'

'Well keep your sense of humour and remain positive. I'll say a prayer for you. Good bye and good luck.'

'Thanks, I will,' I said and headed to the ward on East Wing to start my association with this famous hospital.

East Wing had been completely renovated and was newly opened by the Queen in 1990. I took the lift up to the third floor and was greeted by Caroline, the Sister in charge of outpatients.

'So you are going to teach me how to stab myself?'

'That's right. Now the treatment is a combination of the Interferon injections and the chlorambucil chemotherapy tablets. You need to take the tablets every day and give the injections three times a week for the first six weeks. Then only take the injections for the next two weeks before reverting back to the tablets and injections together again. The Interferon must be stored in the fridge. We will make an appointment for your next blood test before you leave because we need to check on your blood count regularly. Please telephone if you have any problems and remember not to push it as the drugs will make you tired and weak. Luckily your lovely red curly hair will not be affected this time but I will give you medicines for your mouth as it is the first area to get infected. I have two bags ready for with dozens of needles, one of which is to draw the water to mix with the Interferon, the other for the injection, swabs, bottles of Interferon, water vials and a needle dispenser.'

Madge invited me to stay in her house during the first few weeks so that she could help and keep an eye on me. Her son, Ian, was away at boarding school but her daughter, Catherine, was there. Catherine was in secondary school at Saint Mary's where I had worked with Alison, Simone and Steve in the P.E Department.

After a short rest I took the tablets with some food and prepared the Interferon. I went into Ian's room and nervously injected myself. Then I sat down with Catherine and Madge to watch the television and wait to see what would happen. Caroline had described the type of side-effects to expect but as each hour passed I became more concerned that nothing was happening. Maybe it was not working. How wrong I was!

At about one o' clock in the morning the first attack struck. I suddenly started to shake violently in the bed, shivers ran up and down my spine and my head began to pound like crazy. Despite covering myself with several more blankets a dreadful chill gripped me. Then the terrible sickness hit me. I felt as if I had been poisoned and I became violently ill.

Madge came to my aid but there was nothing she could do. It was awful. My head was absolutely pounding with a piercing pain, yet I could not stop being sick. My body jerked and heaved as if possessed. I was sweating profusely, totally drained, and my stomach was very sore from the contractions and dry heaves. Just as I started to regain control the next wave came, and then the next and the next.

Five hours passed before any respite. Five hours of vomiting and sweating and pain. It was sheer hell. I had never experienced anything like it and a terrible fear gripped me as I thought of the future. How could I conceivably go through this, day in, day out, week after week? Enervated, feeble and weakened beyond belief, I lay in the bed moaning in self-pity.

Three days passed and I was in such a poor state that I had to return to the hospital and get stronger anti-sickness and painkiller tablets. The new drugs helped somewhat and eventually my life began to calm down. I was still very weak, especially after the rough start, but I soon settled into a routine. I took my anti-sickness and chemotherapy tablets every day and injected myself with the Interferon on Mondays, Wednesdays, and Fridays. At the peak of my athletic days, my body fat was seven percent. Now that I had to inject myself, I found that my stomach was the best place for the injections. Usually I had to force myself to stick the needle in, but somehow, after hours of procrastination, I managed to do it. Madge kept the house impeccably clean, sterilising everything, and my strength returned slowly. I was relieved to be feeling better but my introduction to the powers of chemotherapy had not been a pleasant one.

My regular visits to Barts continued, as it was imperative to keep checking the effects that the chemotherapy was having on my blood counts. If the results showed that my levels had dropped too low, then I stopped the treatment until my counts rose again. By now I knew a lot of the nurses, doctors and patients on the ward as well as the team of administrative staff, including Debbie and Susan who made the appointments for me.

At the end of March, four and a half weeks after I had started the treatment, I returned to work. Being a schoolteacher and interacting with kids meant that it was almost impossible to avoid colds and viruses but I managed without any problems. Initially it was tough because my energy levels were so low but I was delighted as it was a big psychological boost to restore some sort of normality to my life.

Despite this achievement, I missed my

running. I hoped that I would soon be able to start training again. Just as in my youth, I now felt guilty about not running and highlighted the page in frustration. It was the psyche of the athlete to push himself day after day and I was desperate to get back to it. It was ingrained into my system that for every day out of training I lost two days and it really bothered me how my fitness was suffering.

For the next three months I pressed on diligently with my routine of drugs and injections until finally I finished the course and Peter booked a scan and a bone marrow test in order to assess the situation. I knew that there was no point in worrying too much about the future. I did not want to drive myself crazy thinking about all the different possibilities. I had to live each day as it came. The only certain thing was that the bone marrow test had left me sore and bruised.

On 22 July, after six months of using my stomach as a pincushion, I returned to Barts to talk to Dr. Rohatiner, who was the senior consultant with Professor Lister. She told me that the treatment had worked well, and the lumps in my stomach were smaller. However, they would now have to try more aggressive treatment which would be more debilitating and would also make all my hair fall out. Stronger chemotherapy meant there would be a higher risk of infection and that I would have to be careful in the school. We agreed to start on 31 August to give me a short break.

Naturally I was disappointed but I had realised that this was always a possibility and I was prepared to fight on. Apart from the disappointing news and the worry about my job, I realised I would now have to tell my Dad. When I became ill, I looked to my family for inspiration and encouragement and I could not have had a better role model than my Dad. He was shocked by his illness but because he was a fighter he eventually came to terms with it and against all the odds he slowly started to fight back.

In early August 1993 I went to Ireland before the start of my second stage of treatment. Dad was making progress and he had now survived for ten months. Normally going home was a very happy occasion but this time it was different. This was the moment the whole family had been dreading. We had all been living under terrible pressure and now at last all was to be revealed. Although I was worried, I realised that there was no alternative because once my hair fell out it would be obvious that something was wrong. Dad had the right to know about my illness and I needed him now. The strain on the rest of my family in Ireland in trying to hide the truth from him was immense. He had improved to the extent whereby we hoped that he was strong enough to deal with the news. It had to be now and I was the one who had to do it.

I planned to stay at home for two weeks before returning to England to start the new chemotherapy. I wanted to tell Dad the very first night so that we would all have plenty of time to talk about it and to help him come to terms with the inevitable shock.

My father was sitting in his chair in their new

conservatory looking out at the beautiful view of the lakes and mountains. Mam and Dad's house in Roundwood was the perfect place for him to convalesce. The tranquillity and the beautiful, quiet countryside was, as he said himself, his little piece of heaven.

'Hello, Dad, I'm home.'

'Hi son, welcome back' he replied and then kissed me.

'How are you feeling, Dad?'

'I'm grand son, losing weight, but time's the healer.'

John arrived in with the bags. He had supported Manchester United from boyhood, whilst I was a Gunner and had always supported Arsenal. My poor Dad was always caught in the middle and whenever we were all together we would have great debates about the games. Not just football for, along with me, both John and Dad were great sports lovers-golf, rugby, football, athletics, whatever was on.

'Hi Dad,' John said. 'Did you see the football last night? That was a great goal in the second half. What a beauty!'

'Sure, he was a mile offside,' I said when John's back was turned and winked at my Dad.

'What?' howled John, 'he had a yard to spare! What did you think, Dad?'

'I don't know, son,' said Dad; 'it was very close.'

'Come on you lot,' called Mam, 'sit down and have a cup of tea. Mark is tired'

'Yes you look tired,' said my Dad quietly.

We all sat, even though I pretended not to hear my Dad's comment. I did not need any reminders that although physically he was weak, his mind was sharp as a razor and he had already noticed that I was tired. John stayed for two hours and then had to go home. I saw him out to his car.

'Are you going to talk to Dad later?'

'Yes.'

'I'll come back up tomorrow night and see him then.'

'Thanks for getting me from the airport. Say hello to Norah for me.' Norah was John's girlfriend and was a nurse in Dublin.

I went back inside to find Dad already in his bed. He usually did that around half past seven and sat up reading or watching the television. Mam said that Ruth had rung and would come up later. It was now or never. I went to his bedroom.

'Okay, Dad?'

'Fine, Mark, tired, but I'm getting a little better each day. I'm not bad for an auld fellah.'

'It's great to be in Roundwood. It's so beautiful.'

'Sure it's heaven all right and I have a lot of interests to keep me going. The other day a man told me that I was great because if he had been that sick he would taken a load of pills and ended it all. I told him he ought to be ashamed of himself talking like that. Going out to the garden and doing a little bit is great and if I cannot walk then I'll go on my hands and knees, or I'll crawl, and if I cannot crawl I'll get a wheelchair.'

'Good for you. I have that attitude myself.'

There was silence for a while as the noise from the TV drifted in and out of my consciousness. I took a deep breath. I had no idea what to say but I just had to say something and get it off my chest. The only other time I found myself in such a difficult situation was when I came home to tell my parents about the break up of my marriage. That had been very difficult but this was worse; this was on a totally different plane all together.

'Dad, I have to talk to you about some bad news.'

'Oh. What's wrong?'

'I'm sick,' I replied. 'I have been sick for quite a while and I never told you. I'm sorry!'

'What kind of sickness, son?'

'I...em,' and then, damn it, then it happened. I started to cry. Shit, just at the wrong time.

'Does the mother know?'

'Yes. It all happened when you were very sick and I was afraid to tell you because you were so ill. I am sorry.'

'That's okay, son, no harm done, I'm fine now. What actually is wrong with you?'

'It's called lymphoma and I just woke up one day with a lump on my neck and it all started from there.'

I got up from the bed and started walking around the room. It was all going wrong. My voice was shaking and I was scared and worried that I would frighten him too much. Through nervousness I blubbered on about tests and lumps being removed and lumps in my stomach and in my neck. It seemed that all I was saying was lumps, lumps, lumps.

The walls of the room closed in on me and I wanted to run out of it. I loved my Dad so much and here I was telling him dreadful news, news that could only make him sad. But I went on and on through the tears.

'I have had chemotherapy also,' I said.

Chemotherapy! The word sounded like poison,

it smelt of fear and was an admission that my illness was serious.

'What are they going to do for you now, and where?'

'Well, I need to start some new treatment in two weeks and then, in about four months, they will test me again to see how things are going. I'm attending a very famous hospital called St Bartholomew's-it's in London-and they are experts in treating this kind of illness.'

I stopped and wiped my eyes. What a mess I had made of it all. Dad was sitting up in his bed looking so serious and sad. I could feel his pain. Going over to the bed I knelt down, put my head on his chest and cried. He put his arms around me and hugged me tightly. How long I was there crying I do not know. I was lost, alone with my Dad, closer than ever before, hugging each other in the dark of his bedroom.

Later, sometime later, my Mum came into the bedroom and joined us. We talked for about another hour and then Dad fell asleep. We let him rest and chatted in the kitchen. Ruth arrived up later and she went in to talk to Dad and spent about an hour or so in there. The night went on forever. I was emotionally exhausted and drained. Sleep came in fits. Nightmares rushed at me from all angles and in the early hours of the morning I woke terrified by my own dreams. My Dad was worn out the next day. John arrived that night and spent time with him. We were all in the house supporting one another.

Mam & Dad's wedding in Blackrock. Front Row. Dad's brother Tom, Dad & Mam, Mam's sister Dina, Father Finnegan. Back Row. Dad's Father, Mam's Father& Mother, Dad's brother Kevin

The Director's Chair

The Three Musketeers. Ruth, John & Mark aged 11, 7 & 3

Aged 12. Running for Dublin in Liverpool

ALL IRELAND JUNIOR TEAM ATHLETICS JOINT CHAMPIONS 1979
C.B.C. MONKSTOWN & ST.MUNCHINS 25pts; ST.JOSEPHS CROSSMAGLEN &DUNGARVAN C.B.S. 14 pts
LEINSTER : 1st C.B.C.MONKSTOWN 53 pts, GORMANSTON 36 pts ROSCREA 28 pts
" FIELD EVENTS : 1st C.B.C. MONKSTOWN 47pts, GORMANSTON 25, ROSCREA 16pts.
C.B.S.: C.B.C.MONKSTOWN 36pts, ATHY 15pts, ENNISCORTHY 13 pts.
EAST LEINSTER : C.B.C.MONKSTOWN 60pts. BLACKROCK 17 , PRES BRAY

ALL IRELAND SHIELD
EAST LEINSTER SHIELD
LEINSTER TEAM SHIELD
C.B.S. SHIELD
LEINSTER FIELD EVENTS TEAM

1979. Displaying our trophies at CBC Monkstown. I'm top left

What technique! Running the 400 meters hurdles at CBCMonkstown school sports 1980

Leaving for the U.S.A. 1984 . Me, Dad, John & Mam. Why is everyone so happy?

Fighting to the line against athletes from Eastern Kentucky

Finishing in tandem with my room-mate Billy Porter, Tenessee 1984

Tenessee 1985

Dressed for a Miami Vice party. Danny, Steve, Me, Kevin, Jamie

Leading on the boards at the Idaho State Indoor Track

That winning feeling

Kicking hard as leader of the pack entering the last lap. Indoors 1989

Receiving Athlete of the Year award from Dubby Holt and Sam Bennion

Winning the Indoor Big Sky 800 meters title fot the second time. 1989

1987 4x800 meters Indoor relay team. 7.22. New Stadium & Idaho State record. Jeff Jaynes, Rene Sepulveda, Dave Cook, Mark Byrne

Two very proud moments. A lifetime's ambition fulfilled wearing the Irish vest. 1988-1989

Loving parents. Dad and Mam

A Spanish Beauty, Marisa in full flow

Happy Days. Dermot, Ruth, Dad, Mam, John & me (on the floor!)

Mam, Norah, John, Dad & Ruth at John & Norah's Wedding

Happy and laughing in our room at St Bartholomew's during the World Cup in July 1994.

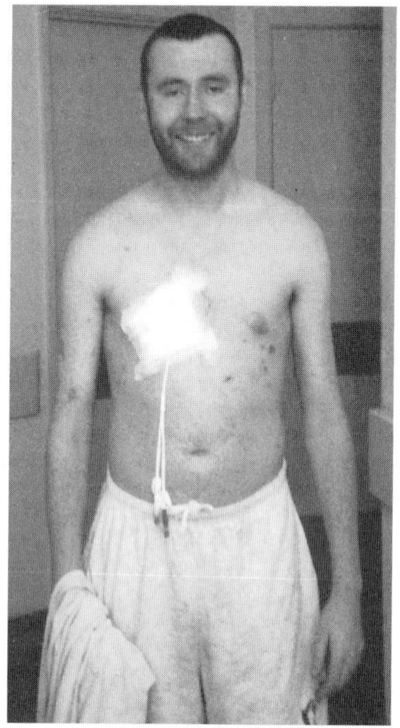

What a body. Hy Hickman line and the efforts of tons of steroids just days after receiving my bone marrow transplant. May 1994

One night I was in my Dad's bedroom when he said: 'Mark, it is when things are really hard that you need to fight back. Nobody likes being kicked in the shins.' I really liked that saying and knew I could use it to inspire me when I needed encouragement. Dad knew that everybody was worried about him and he told me a poem that perfectly summed up his attitude towards things. He had had a lot of operations and setbacks in his own life but had always pulled through and his sense of humour never left him. It was his hallmark, gentle, kind, and funny.

The Shape I'm In

There is nothing whatever wrong with me
I'm just as healthy as can be
Although I have arthritis in both my knees
And when I talk I speak with a wheeze
My pulse is weak and my blood is thin
But I'm awfully well for the shape I'm in
And I think my liver is out of whack
For I have a terrible pain in my back
My hearing is poor and my eyes are dim
And most everything seems to be out of trim
For the way I stagger is a crime
I'm most likely to fall at any time
But all things considered
I'm awfully well for the shape I'm in
My dentures cut and I'm restless at night
And in the morning I'm a frightful sight
Memory is failing, head's in a spin
I'm practically living on aspirin

But I'm awfully well for the shape I'm in
Now the moral is as this tale I unfold
That for you and me who are growing old
It's better to say I'm fine with a grin
Than to tell everybody of the shape we're in

I returned from Ireland relieved that finally my Dad now knew the entire story. My mind was free to focus on what lay ahead and I knew that the words and conversations that I had had with him during those two weeks would live forever in my memory.

7

THE GOOD, THE BAD AND THE BALD

On 31 August 1993 I started the new treatment which was a combination of different chemotherapy drugs called CHOP. I was uncomfortable and nauseous in the hot stuffy room and I had to concentrate really hard to avoid throwing up. Caroline arrived armed with a tray full of equipment. I took a deep breath, trying to relax as she prepared to put a cannula in my wrist.

'A cannula enables us to administer the drugs intravenously so that they are then absorbed quickly.'

The heat of the room and the sting of the needle in my vein made my stomach heave a little but I managed to control myself. My heart was beating faster and faster as I listened to Caroline explaining about CHOP and its side-effects. My armpits were sweating profusely and I prayed that no one would notice how nervous I was.

'This is CHOP. It is stronger chemotherapy than your first lot and it will have greater effects on you. I'll give you an anti-sickness drug in the injection to help when the effects hit.'

Looking up, I saw a very large syringe full of a red dye liquid. 'Hit,' I said somewhat panicking. 'I hope that I make it home before the fun starts.'

'You will be fine. The effects will not come for about four hours. Now, the major side effects of CHOP are that you lose your hair from your head and body. This is naturally a hard thing for some people to deal with.'

'I will wear a bandanna with a sports cap that I usually have anyway. Most of the students know that my hair is going to fall out, so it will not be a problem.'

Caroline finished with the CHOP and picked up a new one.

'Now this drug has to be given slowly. If you start to feel a little hot and sweaty or a burning sensation in your bottom, then I need to know as the drug is going in too quickly. The school environment is not ideal as CHOP can really lower your white blood cells and your ability to fight infections. If you feel unwell or get a cold, call us immediately. I'll also give you mouthwashes and lozenges to keep your mouth free of ulcers and blisters.'

'And the injection will help with the nausea?'

'Yes, but unfortunately, despite the advances in medicine, losing your hair and nausea are still real problems associated with chemotherapy.'

Getting the treatment was an uncomfortable experience despite the cheerful nature of the nurses joking and encouraging us. In all, the whole process of getting the drugs and fluid took about an hour and a half. By the time it was finished, I was drained and ready to go home. I was told that I should expect the sickness to last at least three to four days which meant that I would need more days off work to recover. Walking out of the doors of the hospital into the cold sharp air, I was overcome with a great sense of relief and freedom. The fresh air helped suppress the nausea in my stomach. It felt so good that I just stood there, eyes closed, enjoying the moment.

The train journey back was okay and on arrival at the school I went to my rooms to relax a little before the night's excitement began. It was very strange knowing that in an hour or two I would be violently ill and that I had better make the most of the time while I could.

When the terrible sickness hit, I had my little red basin ready. I was prepared for the ordeal, alone in my own rooms. It was best that way. My way of dealing with the nausea was to convince myself that this was all for the best, that it meant that things were working. The more I vomited, the more badness was going out of me and the closer I was to a cure. I told myself to remain calm, confident and defiant, that life would improve no matter how difficult and miserable it seemed right now.

I was pouring sweat and lay on the floor absolutely drained and wrecked. I kept hoping that it would all pass but no sooner did I think it had done so than the sickness returned. The attacks lasted about four hours before gradually subsiding, leaving me weak and exhausted. Caroline told me to expect the effects to last a few days, so I took Monday, Tuesday, and Wednesday off work. By Thursday I felt strong enough to return to work but not strong enough to run yet. I had a glowing red complexion from the drug, and the staff joked that I had been away getting a tan and that I was not sick at all.

Three weeks after the first injection I returned to Barts for the second injection. Being back in the hospital was not a very pleasant experience but I knew that it was for my own good. The routine was the same as before, involving a blood test and then a long wait in the Oncology Clinic to see Dr. Johnson. As part of every visit, I lay on a table for him to examine me. He felt around all the main lymph gland areas, which included my neck, under my arms, around my groin and my stomach, as well as checking my blood pressure and listening to my breathing. Peter then phoned to see if my blood counts were high enough to receive more chemotherapy. They were okay and so I went for the injection and after a long tiring day I finally headed back to the school.

I drank a milk build up and had some plain biscuits because I was hungry from the hours at the hospital. I prepared for the sickness as I had done before with the little red basin, a cloth, and water to wash my mouth out. When the cramps began, I told myself to be strong. On my hands and knees I started to throw up. The poison had begun but I needed it and so, in a strange way, welcomed it. Wave after wave of nausea, alone, lying on the floor of my rooms being sick for untold hours. My stomach muscles ached from the exertions as if I had performed a thousand sit-ups. Luckily the next day I threw up only twice, despite feeling very queasy and by Thursday I was well enough for work. Tired as I was, it was a relief that the horrors were over for another few weeks.

Two weeks later I went to the X-ray department at Barts for a scan to see if the lymphoma was responding to this more aggressive approach. I drank some liquid an hour before the scan and then I lay on a table that moved inside a big cylindrical machine where the X-rays were taken. It was a painless experience, which lasted about forty minutes.

On 18 October I returned to Barts to get the scan results. Naturally I harboured hopes that this might be the end of it all but they were soon dashed when Peter informed me that the lumps were still there and that I should continue with the chemotherapy. Disappointed, I accepted my fate and vowed to fight on.

When I arrived back to the school, I was delighted to see my friend Brent Caudill from America. Four eventful years had passed since we had last seen each other and even though we had kept in contact, we still had a lot to catch up on. Brent stayed around for about ten days and his good looks caused quite a stir with the girls and some of the female staff. It was great to see him again and it gave me a real boost, but all too soon he was gone.

My hair started to come out towards the end of the fourth injection. Michele McNamara worked as a Physical Education teacher on the girls' side at the school and we were good friends. We always joked and looked on the bright side of my situation. She even contemplated buying a wig for me as a joke as she had the same zany, weird sense of humour that I had.

'Do you know where is the first place that I

have noticed hair falling out from?' I asked her one night.

'Where?'

'Down there,' I said pointing to my groin. 'I'm as bald as a chicken there, nothing left. And look at this!'

With that I grabbed a huge clump of hair on my head and pulled it clean off.

'Oh my God. Didn't that hurt?'

'No, it's dead hair. Here! You have a go.'

'No way, you have a big bald patch now at the back. Go and show Steve for the laugh. That's outrageous.'

Steve Gibbons lived next door to Michele, so we made a plan to trick him and headed for his room.

'Hello, Mark, how are you feeling?'

'Oh, all right, Steve, but Michele is annoying me.'

'I just told him that if he does not drive the mini-bus and go out to matches in bad weather it's going to cause huge problems for the kids and me.'

'Look, I can't help it if it rains. What about my immune system?'

'Oh, come on, Michele,' implored Steve.

'Don't worry, Steve,' I said putting my hands on my head, 'I'm totally fed up with the whole thing.'

With that, whump! I pulled a lump of hair out in my left hand. Before anyone spoke, I tugged a second lump out with my right hand. I stood holding two big wads of red hair. I did not look at Michele for fear of laughing. Steve's face was pale and shocked. His mouth dropped wide open.

'I told her not to annoy me. Now I'll have to get rid of it all,' I stammered and started pulling more hair out.

'Oh! Stop please!' cried Steve, but it was too late. Michele and I were on the ground laughing in tears; for once the pain in my stomach had nothing to do with chemo.

Teaching and walking around the school with my bandanna and sports cap on was strange at first, but I, and everybody else, soon got used to it. The weeks passed and my approach of welcoming the sickness helped me to deal with it. Overall I was proud that I had managed to continue teaching. My goal was to control my illness as much as possible and not let it control me. By continuing to work and train on the days when I had enough energy, I felt I was beating the cancer. I did not ignore my illness, but I did not want it to change my lifestyle. My approach was to look on the bright side of life, as it was the only way that I could survive and remain sane.

At last my diary pages were slowly beginning to take on a familiar look. Instead of details of how many times I had been sick or what my blood count was, I could now write that I had been for a five mile run or had completed some sort of workout on the track. Running played a crucial part in keeping me going. I refused to let any thoughts of never racing again enter my head. I had too many good memories to let that happen and on the nights when I was alone and feeling sad, I took out my scrapbook and reminded myself of the good times.

Running was in my blood, chemotherapy or no chemotherapy. I had a passion for it and I constantly thought about special times such as the emotional build up to a race when I had to go away on my own for up to two hours before it to prepare myself mentally. I could see races in my head, feel the power when I ran and the ecstasy of winning. I knew what it was like to race against Olympic Champions and medallists like Earl Jones, Joachim Cruz, and Paul Ereng; what it was like to race in front of twenty thousand people, to represent my country and hear the Irish National Anthem, 'Amhráin na bhFiann'.

I had run countless miles, repeat 200 and 400 metres around the track until my lungs almost exploded, trained in the pouring wet rain and at altitude in the cold dry air of the Rocky Mountains. I had experienced the incredible buzz of kicking hard off the last bend and flying past opponents to win important titles and receive the congratulations of my teammates. I had followed my dreams, challenged myself both physically and emotionally and succeed by hard work and dedication. They were my achievements, my life, and, I was not, at just twenty-nine, going to let any cancer take that away from me.

In late September I met Marisa, who had recently arrived at the school from Spain, and immediately we hit it off. Her bubbly, lively attitude and sense of humour lifted me, and I found myself spending ever more time with her. I was amazed at the way that she took the news of my illness and problems completely in her stride. It astonished me that, at the most vulnerable phase in my life, someone was willing to put aside my marital and health problems to be with me.

I continued to teach and I was proud of the fact that I could still play rugby and run. My desire to control my illness and to surround myself with people who were outgoing and positive continued at the local pub. It proved an ideal venue to release any pent-up frustrations and, along with a half dozen people who taught and worked at St Edmund's, we had many a good session there. The A Team was formed and we would sit around debating and voting on our top five movies, songs, actors or actresses.

It was an innocent but quite necessary outlet for me where I indulged in a few pints of cider every now and again. One night I mentioned that I was writing a book about a mercenary called Bubba, set in Manila in 1962, and the different characters he hung out with. Within minutes they all wanted to be a character and I spent the night writing down what their drunken minds conjured. I had fifty cards printed with 'The A Team' and 'Manila 62' on them. This period between chemotherapy was a pleasant, enjoyable time and as Marisa worked most nights doing boarding duty, increasingly I ended up there seeing her.

At half term I went home to be with my parents. Dad was making slow progress and Mam did her best to encourage him. It was a great boost for them to have me home, even though initially they were shocked to see me bald. My Dad had lived for one year now since his operation and we were all amazed at his strength and determination. Mam's boundless energy combined with Dad's steely will made a formidable team. Weak though he was, he still went to eight o' clock mass every morning.

Whilst I was there, I went out with the lads several times. Once I met Tom, Dermot, Dick and Jamie in Stillorgan for a few drinks before heading across the road to the Bowling Alley. We were all in high spirits and it must have been the combination of the chemo, the baldness and the alcohol because I was hot at the bowling. Strike after strike followed until Jamie made a late burst for the title of hot shot. Afterwards we went to a chipper. Half-pissed, I smiled to myself as we sat on a wall in the freezing cold eating the food. I was drunk but happy.

'I really enjoyed tonight,' I proclaimed loudly.

'It's great to see you looking so well,' replied Tom.

'He's a baldy git,' said Jamie.

'So are you still on chemo?' asked Dermot.

'Yes and I am freezing out here with no hair on my head or me balls. I am the Kojack of Kojacks.'

They erupted with laughter, half-choking on their chips.

'Of course the worst part is when you have to have a dump; loads of hair comes out in the shit.'

'Jayzus, Byrner, 'I'm trying to eat, roared Dermot.

'I'm only letting you know how lucky you are,' I replied and staggered off laughing.

'And to think he never drank for twenty-eight years,' added Jamie.

I returned to England for the last six weeks before Christmas. Out on the rugby pitch one day a student accidentally sent me crashing to the ground. My hat went one way, my bandanna the other, and the whole class gasped, as I lay there bald and helpless. Quickly I was helped to my feet in silence.

'Well,' I began as I retied my bandanna, 'I must be slowing down in my old age. It must be the chemo and I thought it would make me more aerodynamic. Good tackle, well done,' and I charged off up the pitch to restart the game.

Of course, the main advantage of my situation was that I was allowed to wear my hat and bandanna, even in the parlour. The parlour was strictly for the teachers and had certain rules and dress codes when staff were eating there. I, however, was exempt because of the treatment and wore my headgear in there and all over the school. Some of the kids thought I looked like a rock star.

Marisa and I started going out with each other in November and as the Christmas holidays arrived, it looked as if the year would end on a high. Fate, however, had other plans. The week before Christmas, as most families were preparing for the festive celebrations, we were devastated by news of my sister Ruth. I was at home from school holidays when she discovered a lump at the side of her breast, which was diagnosed as breast cancer. It was in the early stages but immediately her doctors set up a programme for treatment. An operation to remove the lump was booked for early January and then a course of chemotherapy and radiotherapy for an initial period of six months.

Bewildered and shattered, we collectively were at a loss to explain our misfortune. Within that fourteen-month period, three out of five members of the family were diagnosed with three different types of cancer. Dad's was in his stomach, Ruth's in her breast, and mine in my neck and stomach. As a family unit we united with Ruth's own family in support of one another at such an untimely and cruel coincidence. What else could we do but to put aside our individual problems and encourage each other that life would improve and soon the tide would turn for the better.

Before I returned to England, I went to Melilla to visit Marisa and her mother Margarita. Margarita welcomed me with open arms and pampered me from the minute I arrived. Unfortunately, she spoke no English and I had no Spanish, so we were limited to sign language and Marisa's constant interpretative skills especially when Real Madrid were playing on the television. It was the perfect break before heading back to the hospital for the scan results after such a dreadful year.

8

ALL ROADS LEAD TO BARTS

Nineteen ninety-four began with a visit to St Bartholomew's almost a year to the day since I discovered the lump on my neck. As I sat in the clinic awaiting the results of the latest tests, the various possible and probable permutations flashed around in my head. Mind games can be a terrible torment but I tried to dispel the infinite questions and words like cure, treatment, and cancer, which bounced around my head pinball style. The clinic was packed with patients, and as I looked at them, young and old alike, I realised that they were probably all having similar thoughts. It seemed that everyone was grappling with the why and what ifs that life throws up. Eventually, after a very long wait, I went in to see Professor Lister.

He informed me that even though the lumps in my stomach were much smaller, he was not quite convinced that they had gone completely. The scans can apparently be quite difficult to interpret because of what might be scar tissue. He wanted to try another chemotherapy drug to see if anything changed. This new drug was called fludarabine and I was to start it the following week.

The Professor explained that the problem was that my lymphatic system was infected. This meant that a particular type of white blood cell present in the lymphatic system, called a lymphocyte, which also gathers in stations around the body known as lymph nodes, must have become cancerous. It is when this happens that it is called lymphoma. The lymphatic system is like the blood system and can unfortunately help spread the cancer throughout the body to the various lymph nodes. It can then affect how those organs function and it's this uncontrolled growth of cells that can infect two or three areas.

Nobody could tell me if I had a good chance of being clear soon, and, if so, how long that would last. Neither could they say if the lymphoma would ever return in the future or not because each individual case was so different and no one individual reacted in the same way to the illness or the treatment. He then explained that in my case because of my age and the details of my illness, that my best chance of defeating the lymphoma would be to have a bone marrow transplant.

It was now obvious that after the next set of treatment and results I should have a bone marrow transplant. I was a little shocked at the thoughts of a transplant. Everything was happening so fast. I was worried about my Dad and Ruth who was starting chemotherapy, and also worried for John, Mam and Marisa. It was a lot for one family to handle and I wondered where it was all going to end.

I felt that I had coped incredibly well so far. I knew that my age and mental toughness would be an enormous advantage to me and that the best thing to do was to concentrate on myself. I hoped that when my loved ones saw me doing well, then they would be encouraged to fight on in a similar manner.

Dr. Anand, in Buntingford Health Clinic, was my GP and I went there to get the new injections of chemotherapy. Fludarabine thankfully had few side-effects. Every day for five days I drove to Buntingford for an injection; then I waited for three weeks, had a blood test and started again with the five-day course. I managed fine on the treatment and just got on with life as best I could.

In April I returned to Barts for more scans and a meeting with the professor, where it was decided to go ahead with the bone marrow transplant. Everything had been worked out and Professor Lister went through the itinerary with me. A week before going into hospital I had to give myself some G-CSF injections to help stimulate my bone marrow to push cells into the peripheral blood for collecting. I had to start the injections on 27 April for five days then return to Barts on Monday 2 May for the actual harvest. The procedure of collecting the marrow was called 'Harvesting' and the injections were to ensure that there would be enough cells available for the transplant.

Under a general anaesthetic they would take a litre of bone marrow, about twenty needle holes from my back, to store until after the treatment. The amount of chemotherapy and radiotherapy would be so strong that if some of my bone marrow was not stored beforehand, then the treatment would totally destroy all of my immune system and I would have nothing left to defend again infection or disease.

The treatment would last for five days with

Chemotherapy in the first two days and the radiotherapy for the next three. Chemotherapy is the use of anti-cancer (cytotoxic) drugs that are used to kill the lymphoma cells. The idea was to stop the cells dividing and therefore the cancer growing and spreading. Radiation treated cancer by using high-energy rays to kill the cells. The chemotherapy of cyclophospamide and TBI referred to the radiotherapy part of the treatment, that is 'Total Body Irradiation' and ABTM is an Autologus Bone Marrow Transplant. It was called an 'Autologus Bone Marrow Transplant' since I was receiving my own marrow back. The actual medical term was 'Cyclophosphamide + TBI + ABMT.' Once the heavy treatment was over, I would then receive back my marrow cells. After that it is a case of wait and see and hope that everything worked.

He told me that I needed to go to the radiotherapy lab to meet the doctors and lab technicians there. They would measure me for the radiotherapy and do some marking on my body. He also made an appointment for me to return to Barts the following Monday to have a Hickman Line put in. A Hickman Line is a plastic tube connected to a large blood vessel near the heart with two smaller tubes branching out of the main line out of your chest. It is through one of these that the doctors administer drugs, blood, and platelets. It would save my veins a great deal.

'Well the sooner we get started the better,' I told him after we had discussed everything.

'Lastly we need to do another bone marrow test, so I have booked an appointment for you for next week.'

'I really hate them. No matter what doctor does it and no matter how much they confess to being the best at doing it without causing pain, it always hurts. Any time someone sticks a needle in you, it hurts, especially when they are breaking off a bone marrow sample.'

'If it's any consolation, Mr Byrne, I have had one done and I sympathise with you. But for now do you understand what the schedule will be and what to expect?'

'Yes thanks,' I answered and I got up to leave.

'I hope all goes well, Mr Byrne.'

'Thanks very much for all your help.'

After lunch I went for a walk to get some fresh air and to gather my thoughts. At two o' clock I headed for the radiotherapy lab. A receptionist handed me a gown and guided me to the changing rooms. Once I was ready I was then shown into a large cold room where the technicians Dave and Karen greeted me. I lay on my back on a table and they measured me from head to toe and marked parts of my body with a water-proof blue pen.

'These markings help us when you come to have the treatment and now with the trial run,' Dave told me.

Karen came over to the bed with some bags filled with a jelly like substances.

'These special bags help to spread out the effect of the radiotherapy as certain areas such as your wrists, neck and feet are thinner than the rest and everything has to be even.'

Karen placed the bags under my armpits and around my neck. My head was taped and strapped down and some belts were fastened around my waist and feet. They placed more bags between my legs, groin, and sides and instantly I felt sympathy with people in the Inquisition. When I was well and truly packed down and secured, they both disappeared to take more readings.

I lay on my side, facing the huge machine that would fire the beams of radiotherapy. Even though I knew that during the radiotherapy I would feel no pain, the whole room, and especially the space age machine with the ray gun on the end of it, looked ominous and imposing. They moved my position a few times and finally after a long tiring day we left for the school.

Marisa informed the school that she would be leaving to stay with me in the hospital. All we had to do then was say goodbye to some friends and kids and prepare for the hospital. I had no idea when I would return to teaching, because not even the medical experts knew what the future held.

May 2 arrived and I went to Barts with an overnight bag. I felt weird and uncomfortable sleeping in the hospital that night as normally my rooms at the school were very quiet and dark; yet here I could hear sirens wailing, buzzers going, the telephone constantly ringing and there were lots of lights on. The plastic pillows were hard and made my neck sweat, and the sheets were uncomfortable and itchy. Worst of all, however, were the moans and groans I sometimes heard from a suffering patient. Realism dawned that this was what my Karma had in store for me.

Athlete one minute, patient the next. My confidence was shaken but I was determined to fight on. Sleep was impossible, so I psyched myself up just like I had done before a race. I told myself how tough I was, how hard I had trained, the races I'd won. I'm only twenty-nine. Of course I'd make it and so would Dad and Ruth.

Early the next morning, Junior, a Jamaican porter with massive dreadlocks, arrived with a wheelchair. We chatted about Bob Marley and reggae music as he pushed me across the square. He was a very philosophical and calm character but all too quickly we arrived at the theatre. When I woke up I was back in my room and Marisa was beside me. My head was really groggy. I threw up into a bowl for ages and felt completely drained. My back was killing me where the holes had been made to take the bone marrow. Two big white pads covered the areas and I felt as though a bull had run over me.

The next day Madge brought us to St Edmund's. We were both exhausted and depressed. That night we made a crazy decision to go to Málaga the next day as we realised that it would be the last opportunity for some time. The weather in Spain was glorious. Tapas and wine on the sea front, walks along the beautiful beach and long lazy evening watching the fishermen mending their nets. We were filling up on last minute memories to help us through the times ahead. I wanted it to last forever.

Inevitably, of course, Monday arrived and we returned to St Bartholomew's. The Hickman Line was booked for eleven that morning, and as we held hands going in the door we realised that time had caught up with us.

When I came round from the anaesthetic, I was violently ill yet again. As I was being sick, Noola and Nicola arrived to take blood to store my bone marrow in. Vicky and Claire then arrived to give me blood and all I could see was blood going in one end and coming out the other. I continued to vomit and occasionally raised my head, groaned and puked some more. It was an awful introduction to what the future might have in store for me. It also clearly demonstrated that once I was a patient, the nurses and doctors would continue to do their jobs no matter how ill I was, and whether I wanted it or not.

After a restless night I was let out the next day with instructions on how to look after the two plastic tubes which now dangled from my chest. Supplied with gauzes, bandages, needles, cleansing liquid, and painkillers, I was told to be back on Friday night. We went to a hotel for the weekend and tried to relax before it all started.

9

WHO ARE YOUR INFLUENCES?

With the passing of one year and the beginning of a new one, I reflected of my life of nearly thirty years. I had an unknown future to look forward to with the rapidly approaching transplant, yet a good deal of experience to draw from. My red hair had returned with a flourish, if somewhat darker and straighter than before. On paper my statistics looked impressive. At 5'11" I weighed ten stone four and I was still very fit, with a resting heart rate of about fifty. I was a non-smoker, non-drinker for twenty-eight years, and my blood pressure was 120/60. Overall I was proud of the shape I was in. I felt ready for the challenge and a new stage in my life.

Dad, Ruth and I were all determined in our own different ways to control our illnesses and live as full a life as possible. I continued as a teacher up until the last possible moment as a deliberate attempt to remain positive and in command of my life. In Roddy Doyle's novel, *The Commitments*, Jimmy Rabbitte asked the question 'Who are your influences?' to people who came to audition for his band. I knew that if I were going to survive the transplant, then it was imperative to draw from my background and experiences.

Anything and everything should and would be used to give me the strength and the attitude necessary to handle the tough days ahead. A definite source of inspiration for me would be my athletics. Over the years I had gained so much from it and it was essential that I used the vast experiences that I had as an athlete to help me cope.

As a teenager, training to get a scholarship to the States, I was inspired by the famous Australian runner Herb Elliott and his eccentric coach Percy Cerutty. Throughout my running career they were some of my heroes because of their philosophies and lifestyle.

Herb Elliott was never beaten over a mile or fifteen hundred metres. He smashed the world record in Dublin on 6 August 1958 by three seconds, cheered on by thousands, including my Dad and his brothers Tom and Kevin. It was the first time in history that five men all ran under four minutes for the mile. Herb went on to win the 1500 metres at the Rome Olympics in 1960 by the biggest winning margin and retired unbeaten at twenty-two.

Cerutty coined the phrase 'Stotan', which comes from the words Stoic and Spartan. His creed was built on a mixture of ideals and practices, of hardness, dedication, mental toughness, love of nature, especially the sea, and creativity. He revolutionised the way athletes ate, trained and lived their lives.

Like Herb Elliott in the 1950s, I was stirred and impassioned by Percy Cerutty's teachings.

Now, at a crucial time in my life, I re-read the book of Herb Elliott's life called *'The Golden Mile'*. It brought back proud and fond memories of my own athletic days and helped me to refocus my mind. I also had books and videos about other great athletes whose different life stories inspired me in my youth and would do so now.

Abebe Bikila was the Ethiopian marathon runner who made history in the 1960 Rome Olympic Games by running the marathon barefoot in a world record time of 2 hours 15 minutes. In 1964 he won again and became the first man to retain the marathon, setting another world record of 2 hours 12 minutes 11.2 seconds, but on this occasion he wore shoes. He did this despite having undergone an appendicitis operation just six weeks earlier. In 1969 he was paralysed in a car accident and, sadly, he died four years later. Emil Zatopek, the Czech runner who had the terrible anguished running style, won gold in the 1948 Olympics at 10,000 and silver at 5,000 metres. Four years later he amazingly won three gold medals at 10,000, 5,0000 and the marathon. These men, along with Ovett, Coe, Walker, Coghlan and Treacy, were my running heroes.

Musically there was Jimi Hendrix, The Doors and James Brown and Bob Marley, plus a host of Irish bands like Thin Lizzy, U2 and Christy Moore. So long as I had music, be it classical, rock or traditional, to listen to, I knew that I would cope. Books, movies, plays and real life stories of people who had overcome all sorts of adversity and tragedy would inspire me. Humour would be supplied by The Marx Brothers, 'Only Fools and Horses' and 'Fawlty Towers'.

As an athlete I had always tried to take something positive from every race and training session no matter how hard it was or how badly I felt I had performed. Be positive, constructive and forward-looking. My own family experiences, and how I had handled the chemotherapy so far, proved that I possessed the right mental approach to survive.

My age and fitness were vital, but so too was the support and encouragement from family and friends in Ireland and England. Ultimately, however, I believed in myself, my will to survive and an enormous confidence that I would make it. At 29 that was the way I was and whether or not I would be good enough only time would tell.

PART TWO

10

ENTER THE DRAGON

The hospital policy allowed for Marisa to sleep on a mattress on the floor and to stay with me twenty-fours a day. There was a fridge, TV and video, plus a telephone in the room. I brought my stereo and a huge collection of videos and music to keep us going. We had only one neighbour, two rooms up, and therefore I could play music without disturbing anyone. There wasn't a great deal of space, but we soon made it our home for what we hoped would be a few quick weeks.

On Friday we went out to see 'Les Miserables'. This was our last night before it all began. We had a magical time, but, like Cinderella, it had to end; all too quickly we found ourselves back on the ward. The doctors warned us how difficult it was going to be and the possible dangers ahead, but I felt confident that I would be okay as Marisa would be with me all the time. These next five days of non-stop bombardment of my body were hopefully going to put an end to the lymphoma and start me on the road to recovery. In essence I knew that the upcoming week was going to be the most important of my life.

Six o' clock sharp on the morning of Saturday 14 May 1994; Geraldine arrived with a deceptively anonymous-looking bag. Neither Marisa nor I had had much sleep and we were both awake and waiting. Within minutes the drugs were coursing through my Hickman Line into my veins. Two hours later I threw up. Even though I was given anti-sickness drugs to try and counter the effects of the chemotherapy, I was still sick. It was always an unpleasant experience, involving either a trip to the toilet or the use of the sick bowl, whichever came first. After chemotherapy I tried to walk down to the kitchen for some toast or cereal and to get out of the room for a break.

Throughout the two days I received regular doses of chemotherapy plus fluids, which meant that I was attached via the Hickman Line to 'Drippy' for most of the time. Trapped, restricted and uncomfortable, I constantly thought of people working on a chain gang and how they felt. Vomiting a lot made me very weak but I was pleased how I had come through the chemotherapy stage. Naturally I found eating a problem because being sick turned me off food, but Marisa encouraged me to keep taking a little at a time and to drink plenty of liquids.

On the third day I went to the Radiotherapy Lab for the start of the TBI. The total body irradiation took place twice a day, once in the morning and once in the afternoon. Marisa and I made our own way across to the X-ray department instead of been taken by a porter, as I wanted to walk to get some fresh air and exercise.

Dressed only in a gown, I was once again strapped down and packed with the jelly bags to help spread out the X-rays. A special glass screen was put in front of the bed and parts of it obstructed with foam type blocks. Karen and Dave regularly checked on me to make sure everything was in order. When they were happy with my position and all the other components, they closed the door and headed to the control room. I was left alone with 'The Gun'. From the control room they could see me on a television monitor and I could talk to them via the intercom system. The actual amount of exposure in a given position was only about twenty seconds at a time but, because I was having full body treatment, the radiographers were constantly in and out of the room moving me around, checking the pen marks and the bags.

Most of the time was spent being moved from one position to another and consequently having to change all the accompanying bags and screen. Naturally both they and I wanted everything to be exactly right. Each session lasted about an hour and fifteen minutes. After the first two sessions I began to feel the effects but we continued to walk to the morning and afternoon sessions because I needed the air to revitalise me from the treatment.

Diary: 17 May 1994. Room 9 Bodley Scott 3 Barts.

Radiotherapy does not hurt and you do not feel anything. It is a strange experience especially having all the jelly bags stuck up between your legs and arms and being fastened in so securely. I felt quite helpless alone in the cold uncompromising room with 'The Gun'. It just stood there big and silent pointing at me. I didn't know whether I should close my eyes or not, pray or just stare defiantly back at it. It would not have looked out of place in the Flash Gordon movie. It is the combination of the radiotherapy and the chemotherapy over the five-day period that is having such a devastating effects on me. Luckily I do not need a bone marrow donor and therefore I am avoiding the risk of my body rejecting the marrow. I hope that the marrow cells will be totally clear when they are put back into me. Then, I wait and pray that they settle down, grow and start to produce blood again. The main thing is to remain focused and confident that I will come through my toughest challenge ever.

At 2.30 p.m. on 19 May 1994 I received my bone marrow cells back. Once connected to the Hickman Line, they took only thirty minutes to be reintroduced into my system. Receiving the cells back was a painless process but my body started to shake and shiver and I'd no idea what was happening. Kirsty arrived to help me.

'These are called rigors. It's a little reaction to the cells. I'll put some stuff through a line here to counteract the shaking and calm you down.'

The cells were yellowish in colour and gave off a really strong smell of sweetcorn, which stank up the whole ward. In about twenty minutes things settled back to normal. This was my first day with my new cells and, in a sense, a new system and I hoped that the little drama of the shakes was not an indication for what lay ahead. The waiting game now began, to see if would recover with my new cells without any complications.

The nurses' station is the fulcrum point to any ward and Bodley Scott three was no different. It was a veritable hive of activity, a non-stop twenty-four-hour action zone. The kitchen was another important place, as patients, their visitors and the medical staff used it twenty-four hours a day. It was well equipped with a large table, six chairs and the facilities to cook, make breakfast, or sit and chat over a cup of tea. The waiting room had a couch, chairs, television and video.

On the ward there was no definitive smell except when a patient received back their bone marrow cells and the whole place stank of sweetcorn. There was one long corridor with twelve rooms for the patients, the kitchen, the waiting room and a couple of administration rooms as well. At each end were the toilets and the storerooms; in the middle, the nurses' station. There was also the cell separator room with three beds in it where some nurses worked gathering and storing platelets. Platelets are small disc-shaped cells that play an important role in clot formation. With a low platelet count, a patient was susceptible to various problems, including nose bleeds, bruising and even haemorrhages. The volunteers were hooked up to a machine that took their blood, separated the platelets out and then returned the blood to the volunteer. It was fantastic to see these people willing to give up their mornings and go to such efforts in order to help others.

We quickly became friendly with everyone on the ward. The first friend we made was Ivan Hargreaves, who had just started his treatment a week before me. He was from Blackburn, but had come from the Christie hospital for a transplant. Prior to the transplant, Ivan, who was a great walker, raised forty thousand pounds for cancer charities by walking from Land's End to John O'Groats. He informed me as to what to expect and so, forewarned, I knew what was coming.

A week later we met Jeremy, who lived in my old town of Bishop's Stortford. He was a big lively character around six three and fifteen stones and was undergoing Stem cell treatment which was similar to a transplant and involved strong chemotherapy and time on the ward. A week after Jeremy came Norman from Lincolnshire. His wife Gill was there looking after him. All the beds on the ward were always full but initially these were our main friends.

We developed into a close group, who, despite our various illnesses, had some very funny times together. It was quite remarkable because, on many a day, roars of laughter and hilarity filled the corridors as we joked, cajoled, and sweet-talked the nurses. Generally we made a nuisance of ourselves. Anything and everything were fair game for our collective wacky sense of humour. Along with the nurses, doctors and the day patients coming and going, life on the ward was as vibrant and homely as it could be under the circumstances. Depending on who was sick or feeling down, the others would descend on their room to cheer them up and to encourage them to keep going.

Naturally, we often talked about our illnesses

and, even though comparing our cancers was somewhat futile, it gave us something to chat about and to focus on. We all realised that each case was different and unique to that individual, but it helped us to bond together and become closer friends. About ten days after the treatment my hair started to fall out again. This was the second time it had fallen out so I did not mind too much. As it was, I felt guilty walking around the ward with a big mop of red hair when everyone else on the ward was bald.

Baldness from the chemotherapy did not discriminate as it affected young and old, male and female, black and white. The 'Bald Brigade' reminded me of an episode in *'Star Trek'*, the original pilot for the series, where the crew came across the blokes with no hair who had the strong mental powers. When I was in America, we called them the 'Cone Heads' or the 'Butt Heads', and now here I was, one of them.

Each morning when I awoke, I found bits of hair on my pillows and in my clothes, which was both irritating and itchy. As an athlete I always had long hair for most of the season, but prior to major Track Championships, or a big race, I would cut it all off. Psychologically it gave me a boost, as I was aerodynamically better, lighter and faster. To continue in the same vein, Marisa and I decided to pluck my hair off and one afternoon we went into the bathroom and plucked all my hair off with our hands. Now I was completely bald, and I was ready to face the challenges that lay ahead. As it happened, I did not have to wait too long.

A doctor named Demetri was the head of 'The Team' now and, with them all in tow, came to explain just how precarious my situation was.

'When you receive a transplant, you are exposed to large doses of agents used to kill cancer cells. The new bone marrow cells take time to produce red cells, white cells, and platelets, and while you are waiting for this to happen, you are devoid of any Immune System. This vulnerable position means that you are highly prone to infections and other complications that can arise.'

My initial problem was my bottom, which really hurt. Using a mirror, I saw that I had a massive sore there. It was not as if it hurt just now and then, but it hurt all the time, especially when I went to the toilet. I dreaded having to go there and wished I were constipated for life. It was so painful sitting there that I put a towel in my mouth and bit on it to prevent my shouting out loud.

Eventually the pain became too great to bear any longer and I told 'The Team'.

Then he arrived! Like a dark foreboding cloud the 'Bum Doctor' came. My worst nightmares come true. To this day I get angry thinking about it. He examined me with as much gentleness, sensitivity and compassion as a male rhinoceros coming home from a hard day at the swamps and finding someone in bed with his partner. When he had gone, I had tears in my eyes and violent thoughts in my head.

Clare was on duty that night and heard of my ordeal. As a joke she pinned a disposable plastic glove to the door, except that it was frozen solid to make a big hand.

Along with the tiredness came the loss of my

taste buds. Now that the effects of the transplant were really kicking in, I completely lost the ability to differentiate between the taste of foods. It subdued my appetite and it was a perplexing and bizarre sensation realising that I now liked and disliked completely new foods because of the change. Professor Lister joked that instead of all the milk build up drinks that I was having, I should resort to some stronger liquids such as Guinness for my iron and weight, whiskey for my white blood cells and red wine for my red cells.

A rash spread all over my body. It was a terrible itch that compelled me to constantly move, scratch and twitch in a desperate attempt to be comfortable. There was no air conditioning in the room and it was so sticky that we had two fans working permanently which made it very difficult to get any sleep because of the noise.

Each morning was identical to the one before. It always started with a 'Terminator' crashing about, followed swiftly by 'The Team'. 'The Team' were the group of approximately eight doctors who did the rounds. On a Tuesday Numero Uno also came. Professor Lister was the main man, and when he came 'The Entire Team' followed close by. The visits did not take long. Glances at my charts, maybe a sarcastic comment or a joke from someone, sometimes a physical examination, and then they left. Adios. Hasta la vista, Baby! Sometimes when 'The Team' came into my room, I was fine but at other times I just lay still, hardly aware of their presence. I knew the routine so well that I let them get on with it, whether it caused me pain or not, whether I cared or not.

I always received a visit from a phlebotomist. A phlebotomist gets a five star rating in my little book which has filled over the years with words which, before my illness, were unknown to me but which are now an integral part of my everyday language. Bram Stoker would have been proud of such a beautiful word for my own private vampire who came morning, noon and night to take my blood. Last but not least were the workers who drilled, banged and swore outside in the hospital grounds. Why they were there I did not know because every day there were rumours that St Bartholomew's was going to be closed. Who said hospitals are for rest?

By ten o' clock we usually made our way down to the kitchen to have a little breakfast and to escape the room. With Marisa's help and attached to my drip stand, which Marisa named 'Drippy', our progress was pedestrian and we would stop and chat with any of the nurses or patients we would meet. The atmosphere was very good. Several of the nurses were from Scotland and Wales and predictably there was always great joking about accents.

The survival game went on twenty-four hours a day. Each day I combated the frustration and fear with humour and defiance. I kicked out however I could. I fought hard to remain positive and focussed. I made myself get out of the bed, the room and not give in. In the words of my father, I planned to 'kick the devil in the shins', to fight back and not to give in.

The great machine that was the hospital trudged endlessly on. Seconds, minutes and hours rolled from one to the next. The noise of 'The Terminators' and the workers outside, 'The Team' on their morning charge, the nurses, the phlebotomists, the cleaners, the tea ladies, the porters, social workers and a dozen others were part of my life every single day.

The happier side of life involved a visit from Jeremy, Ivan, or Norm and Gill, chats in the kitchen with day patients and visitors floating in and out. Madge, Catherine and Ian came regularly, as did Michele, Caroline and Barbara, Sandra and Ciarán, Alison, Phil and Bev. Father Peter was the priest for the hospital. He was in his early thirties, had dark black hair, was about five feet eight and had a pleasant natural personality. Not at all pushy or the lecturing type, both Marisa and I enjoyed his company and frequent visits. Other welcome visitors were Gráinne and Gill, who worked for the social services at the hospital. Both of them offered friendly advice and support for the patients. Friends from both schools, the odd student, and a continuous line of weekend visitors helped to keep us in touch with life outside the hospital.

Marisa used her video camera to capture many memorable moments of Jeremy, Ivan and myself laughing and joking with the various nurses. She also filmed my battered body and shiny head, our decorative room and the daily routine of life on the ward.

Jeremy and Ivan were beginning to feel better by the fifth week as their blood counts returned to more normal levels and were looking forward to leaving the hospital soon. Even though I still felt weak, I hoped I'd be next to go. We began to visit the square on a daily basis to enjoy the weather and escape from the room. It was important for me to walk to try and build up my strength.

One day, while Marisa and I were outside in the square, Jeremy and Ivan arrived declaring that they were going for a drink. The pub was just around the corner and the three baldies and Marisa set off for a pint. Jeremy had shorts and trainers, Ivan and me wore pyjamas and slippers. I could not go in to the pub or mingle with the public because of my immune system, so we all sat outside with our drinks looking like escaped loonies.

Mam, Dad, John, Ruth and Margarita came over to visit whenever possible. Dad and Ruth were coping very well with their own illnesses and, along with Mam and John, we all drew strength from each other's determination. As I walked lap after lap around the fountain with either Marisa or a member of my family, I kept telling myself that I was an athlete again training for a race. It reminded me of all the training I had done over the years in all kinds of weathers and conditions. My life had been dedicated to being as fit and mentally focused as I possibly could be. I compared the tough training regime, when I constantly pushed myself through the pain barrier, to my struggle to get better. The distances and the speeds were different but the mental strength and determination required were the same.

It was inevitable that I compared my fight against cancer, and my desire to live, with my experiences of trying to be a top class athlete. It was my way of dealing with the cancer right from the start and it offered me the best possible chance of succeeding. Day after day I told myself to believe in the people around me and in myself. I knew I had to believe positively that I really would get better and I had faith that I really would survive. Everybody on the ward had their own way of dealing with the problems that can be associated with a serious illness depending on their own personality, background and physical make up. There really was no one special formula that worked and I fell back on my own experiences to help me. I knew that it was my best hope for survival.

11

A SUMMER OF DESPAIR

July 1994 was an extremely hot sticky month. I was thin, bald, uncomfortable, and in hospital. I had no immune system and there was no air conditioning to relieve the soaring temperatures.

I first entered Bodley Scott Three on 8 February 1993 and I came to know it and the hospital, inside and out. Marisa and I were very familiar with everything to do with life on the ward. We had lived in the room for over two months and it was a real struggle. There was no deviation from the routine as the perpetual endless hours dragged on. Every day was a mental battle. We kept each other going and hoped it would all end soon.

Whenever we received a phone call or a visit 'from the outside' it helped to alleviate the boredom and the feeling of being cut off from society. I was weak and tired, yet I was frequently denied the pleasure of a decent night's sleep because I was permanently attached to 'Drippy' and received tablets and injections at the most unsociable of hours. Unable to sleep, I often ended up chatting to the nurses or sitting in the kitchen at three in the morning writing in my diary or just thinking.

The 1994 Football World Cup in America arrived just in time; both Ireland and Spain were in it. I knew I could make it through the next few weeks as three matches were being shown every day until late into the night. The World Cup gave Marisa and me a big lift because we had something else to look forward to, to concentrate on; a great event for everybody on the ward to talk about. The walls of our room were full of get-well cards and letters and we added flags, photographs and banners to turn it into as colourful a display as any Chelsea flower show.

Ireland was the only country from the four home countries to qualify for the tournament and was playing Italy in the opening game. I wore my new Ireland football shirt, shorts, and scarf which Mam and Dad had sent, while Marisa proudly sported the Spanish colours. Ivan, Martin, Norm and Gill all crammed into our room beside Madge and Catherine, Michele, Marisa, Margarita and, of course, me. Several of the nurses and doctors kept coming in and out of the room to see what was happening. Everyone was excited.

Once the game started we all forgot our various problems, finding comfort in a football match thousands of miles away. They say that in times of either anger or huge emotion you can forget all your limitations and do amazing things. There I was, all hot and bothered with basically no immune system to boast about, as bald as an egg, and as physically unfit as I could possibly have imagined. I was sick, tired and could hardly find the energy or enthusiasm to get out of bed and have something to eat.

Then it all changed! Picking up a pass, the main man of famous Irish goals did it again. Ray Houghton turned and struck the most glorious shot up and over the Italian defence, past the keeper, and into the back of the net. Ireland had scored. Gooaal! I jumped higher and longer than Bob Beamon's World Long Jump Record. The whole room erupted as patients, visitors and nurses all clasped each other in congratulations. I almost pulled out my Hickman Line in excitement and then I cried with sheer joy and happiness, wishing I were at home to be part of the craic. Life could not get any better than this. Of course the only problem was that there was still a long way to go and we were all on the edge of our seats, beds and wheel-chairs. I did not want the score to change as I stood to win £68 in a bet, but at the same time I realised that we needed another goal to be safe.

The rest of the time was sheer agony until the whistle finally went. Ireland had won. I will remember that night for as long as I live. It was a great occasion given the circumstances and location of the gathering. There were a lot of very sick people in the room but instantly we all forgot about our problems. Right then no amounts of chemo or drugs could change the fact that we were happy. Happy and normal, at least for a night.

Jeremy left during the sixth week; Ivan and Norm left after eight weeks. Now all the initial crazy gang had gone and a new set of patients was on the ward. We kept hoping that I would get out of the hospital by 19 July, which was going to be my 30th birthday. The reality was that I still required hourly doses of tablets, check ups and regular platelet and blood transfusions.

Some of the lads came over from Ireland to visit because it was Marisa's 27th birthday and it was the last time that I was going to see Steve for some time as he was emigrating to America. They went to a supermarket and arrived back onto the ward with an overflowing trolley-load of food and drink. The nurses were great and allowed us to take over the television room with its sound-proof doors. Together with Jamie, Kevin, Tom, Steve, Dermot, Madge, Ian, Catherine and Michele we had a great party whilst watching Spain against Italy in the quarterfinals of the World Cup. We had a truly memorable time that lifted the spirits of everyone who ventured into the kitchen and television room.

The days dragged on and my blood count refused to rise. Each day when a phlebotomist came to take blood, I asked for an extra neutrophil and a few platelets to be added to my results as I could not leave the hospital until these readings improved. Finally, after ten weeks, we were informed that I could finally go home. I would need to return every few days for some transfusions and a blood test, but I could leave.

I looked at Marisa and her eyes glowed with happiness. We hugged and had a quiet private moment together. We did not speak but it was a hug of thanks, a hug of relief, and a hug of victory. We had won and could now eventually leave.

'Well,' said Marisa, 'I guess we'd better start to clean this place up; that alone will take a day.'

We set about removing posters, banners, and cards from the walls. It felt strange dismantling what had been our home for the past two and a half months. I would be able to celebrate my 30th birthday out of the hospital; I could hardly believe it. Marisa used her video camera to record the historic occasion as we closed the door of our room and walked down the corridor thanking and saying goodbye to everyone. At last the doors of the lift opened and we stepped out into the square. I took a big deep breath and gave a shout of joy.

We settled back into our rooms in St Edmund's feeling a little strange in a new environment. All the students and most of the staff had left on summer holidays. The privacy was sheer bliss. I could now eat when I wanted without booking food a day in advance, sleep in a dark room in a nice bed with proper sheets. Best of all, however, was the peace and quiet. No midnight visits from the nurses, no Terminators, not even a visit from 'The Team'.

We had plenty to look forward to, with only five days to plan my birthday party. I did not have the energy to do very much, and because I still had the Hickman line in my chest, I had to be careful. Just being out of hospital and socialising with people again was fantastic. The birthday party took place in Madge's house and garden, on a beautiful summer's day where we held a barbecue type party. With the help of Ian and Catherine, Madge, Marisa and Michele looked after everything. They turned the place into a vibrant lively fiesta, full of banners, food, drink and music. About thirty friends showed up and, despite the greenfly attacking Jeremy, Martin and me, who were the only baldies present, it was a great success.

Alison and Murray invited us to stay in their house while they went on holidays for a few weeks. It was a lovely house with a huge back garden, so we were naturally delighted as the school was an unsuitable place to recuperate at. At last my life had settled down. Under doctor's orders relaxation and tranquillity were paramount and I was resolute in my determination to enjoy myself. This is what had kept us going through the difficult times. It was a new beginning.

The day we were to go to Alison and Murray's house I felt terrible. My legs and joints were weak, as if I had the flu. As the day progressed, I noticed that the inside of my mouth resembled a minefield. It was covered in blood blisters and this discovery coincided with a constant pain in my left ear. Worried at this sudden setback, just as we were preparing to settle into our new surroundings, I went to a local doctor for some painkillers.

The tablets did not help and in total despair I succumbed to the terrible pain and rang the hospital. Soon I was winging my way back in Madge's car again. Frustrated and in great discomfort, I arrived on the ward disappointed and disillusioned. I did not want to be there, especially since I had been to Barts just two days previously for blood and platelet transfusions, but I had no choice.

The next twenty-four hours were a massive ordeal as my suffering increased significantly. Clare was on duty and she arranged for the night doctor to see me promptly. A young female doctor arrived and took blood samples, temperature readings and a urine sample. She gave me some morphine but, despite this, the pain grew worse with each passing minute. Platelet and blood transfusions arrived and the whole process of being bed bound and attached to 'Drippy' started again. It was an enormous setback and a serious blow to my confidence. After all, it was only three weeks since I had been let out.

After two days the whole left side of my face went numb and distorted. It was like having two separate faces, one normal the other cold and numb. The divide occurred exactly down the middle, from my forehead through my nose, one nostril through the middle of my lips and teeth.

I was informed that the paralysis of my face was called Bell's Palsy. It was caused by damage to the facial nerve or the seventh nerve. Probably because of the pressure from the ear problem; but apart from being uncomfortable and strange, it was not too serious. It would clear.

I went for various scans and X-rays to try and detect what was happening. An ultrasound scan uses sound waves to make a picture. It is a painless experience. They spread gel on the area to be scanned and move a piece of equipment like a microphone over the area producing the sound waves. The echoes are converted into pictures by a computer and I watched the images on a TV screen. They then did a CAT scan. It is another type of X-ray and again the process is painless but takes longer. Also, the most detailed scan was called Magnetic Resonance Imagining, or MRI.

My vulnerable, weak body was transported everywhere in a wheelchair because, not only was I very weak, but also my balance was badly affected. Junior the Rastafarian rapper from Hackney and Pedro who was from Galicia, northern Spain and loved to talk to Marisa, arrived several times for me. We visited too many clinics for me to remember or care about as they took scans from every angle of my head.

I drank some coloured liquid forty minutes before the CAT scan and this dye helped to show up on the X-rays. The MRI scan took about an hour and, despite my having ear pugs, it was very noisy, but painless. I lay on a couch that was moved into a metal cylinder machine. Using magnetism, dozens of pictures were taken which required me to lie very still.

I was taken to the ear clinic for several hearing tests and I threw up in the office of an examining doctor, who was none too pleased. His reaction was one of disgust as if to say 'Oh, a sick person, go away. I am an ear doctor not a puke doctor.' Throwing up for me was almost an art and, despite my poor health, I got pleasure from it that day.

After so many scans I felt that they knew what I was thinking. Some of the nerves associated with my face and hearing were damaged. The various scans showed that there was a blood clot of some sort in my inner ear and this was causing the pain and numbness. They were not certain if the lymphoma or some other kind of tumour had returned and formed in my ear. Another possibility was that a bleed had occurred into the ear and, owing to a lack of platelets a big clot had formed. The clot could have been exerting pressure inside and causing the problems. My platelet count was only two when I arrived and they thought that this probably accounted for what had happened. The paralysis would undoubtedly stop in time but my hearing was damaged permanently. Demetri told me that two top experts would come and see me before a final decision was made.

With that he departed and Marisa and I were left to ponder the news. It was a massive shock about my hearing. My immediate reaction was to think about my teaching and how this would affect it. All I could do was to wait and pray about my ear. Praying had not been my strongest necessity but now I realised I needed its help. Waiting for results and doctors was part and parcel of hospital life but it was still difficult to accept.

The next day a neurosurgeon who specialised in brain and head injuries and worked with seriously injured boxers and crash victims came to visit me. I performed various exercises of balance and coordination for him to observe me and, although I was nervous, I found him to be very kind, professional and thorough. Another doctor arrived to discuss the possibility of laser surgery on the clot if the results showed it to be necessary. His bedside manner was not good but he was no less an expert in his field. The thoughts of a laser beam directed into my ear close to my brain was terrifying. That night brought very little relief as sleep eluded me and my brain worked in overdrive, digesting all that had happened.

Two days later, to my eternal relief, I was informed that it was not a tumour in my ear but a blood clot. Because I had practically no platelets, the bleeding had continued until a large clot formed. I would not need any laser treatment and the clot should eventually break up, returning my face to normal. Strengthened as I was to find out that the lymphoma had not returned, I was bitterly upset to learn that my hearing was damaged permanently. Shaken and withdrawn, I felt utterly deflated.

Diary: 10 August 1994 Bodley Scott 3 Barts.

Mam and Dad rang earlier and I tried to sound cheerful. Sometimes it is too much and they know by the strength of my voice that I am in pain and tired. Today I cried after their call. Sometimes I get very frustrated about my situation and I suppose it's only natural that it will get to me. I hate being here and worrying those who love me.

Performing everyday tasks takes on a whole new perspective when you are ill. Getting out of bed is really hard and so is taking a shower. It takes a gigantic effort and Marisa has to help me to get dry as my energy levels are so depleted. Rita, who is the ward chemist, gave me special cream soap to wash with as it helps with dry and flaking skin caused by the radiotherapy. By forcing myself out of the room and making my body work, I am mentally and physically signalling that I am still fighting; still trying to survive. Every time I leave the room I am winning. The walk down the corridor to the nurses' station is akin to running a marathon for me. My speed might be diminished but my willpower is stronger than ever. I treat the challenge as if it is a race and try to apply the principles of racing in order to succeed.

Psychologically it is good to get out of the room and meet other people on the ward. It helps to remind me that others are suffering also and still battling on. Being told that I am looking better from other patients is like having an injection of a new wonder drug; everyone likes to receive praise and encouragement. Likewise, it is important that whenever we meet another patient we encourage them as much as possible. I believe that in this way strong friendships and bonds develop among many of the patients as they rely on each other for support.

Mam and Dad came over and it gave Marisa a chance to go to Spain to recharge her batteries. It was great to see Mam and Dad, who were both determined fighters. Dad was thinner now but I could see the progress he was making and I took inspiration from that. Ruth had just finished her chemotherapy and radiotherapy and, like me, found it all very tiring. However, she had a very positive attitude and realised the importance of it in helping her recover. She was determined to take her illness head-on and conquer it.

I chatted away to my parents on my daily walks around the square as I tried to build my strength. It was great to be together with them again. I really pushed myself on the walks so as to shown them that I was improving. They would have liked to come over from Ireland more often and stay longer but my Dad's illness and Ruth's own treatment contrived to make that very difficult.

By the end of their stay with me I received news that I was going to be let out in a few days. It was a huge boost for both of them as they headed home knowing that I was getting strong again. At lunchtime on 29 August 1994, I received platelet and blood transfusions and was allowed home.

12

APOCALYPSE NOW

Diary: 30 August 1994. My rooms at St Edmund's.

Every night I go to bed and hope that when I wake up in the morning all my problems will have disappeared. It is the ritual of going to bed to end one day and waking up to a new beginning that keeps me going.

When I awoke the next morning I felt that my mind was seriously playing tricks with me because I could not stand up with the pain in my knees. It was terrible! I tried again and again but with no success. I was paralysed! I rested, calmed myself, took some deep breaths, and after a few minutes tried once more. Sweating with the effort I finally made it and immediately took some painkillers for my knees. Gradually the pain wore off but I was shaken by the experience. When Marisa woke up I told her what had happened but now that the pain had disappeared, we tried to forget about it and hoped for the best.

I went to see the headmaster and he informed me that the school had employed someone until Christmas on a temporary basis. Obviously it was a very difficult situation for both of us, as the school did not know when I would return and they needed a teacher. All we could do was hope that by January I would be strong enough to return.

The rest of the day passed without incident but as I was preparing for bed that night the pain returned. Paranoia had now set in and I felt sure that I was losing my mind. It was my knees again. They stung and ached as if they had been beaten with a baseball bat. Tears gathered like storm clouds as I fought the vicious pain and finally, at one in the morning, we rang the ward. By that time I was reeling in agony and inevitably they told me to return.

Madge and Catherine took us back to Barts. It was 2.00am on Tuesday 31 August; less than thirty-six hours after leaving my room at Barts I was back in it. Unlike the first time, when I had entered the ward full of enthusiasm and confidence, now I made my entrance in a wheelchair, with tears streaming down my face from the excruciating pain. Margaret and Geraldine were on duty and they soon arranged for some morphine.

From 1 May until 1 September 1994, a total of 123 days, I had spent ninety-three of them sleeping in the hospital, with another five days visiting it for scans or blood tests or transfusions. Ninety-eight days is 14 weeks, that is in total 2,304 hours in the hospital or, even worse, about 138,240 minutes. No wonder I was despondent.

The spasms struck again at 5.30 am and an urgent call went out for more morphine. My life was one of agony and torment. The pains were back, attacking my joints. My knees began to ache and gradually the pain intensified to such a degree that they totally seized up. However, bad as it was, worse followed when the searing pain progressed down my shins to my ankles and encompassed the whole of my legs. I was possessed by a terrible parasite drilling away inside my body and regular doses of morphine failed to quash my screams of anguish. I cried like a little baby who is in pain but cannot explain what is wrong. I wailed and moaned and sobbed, clutching my knees in despair.

I was so tired yet, whatever it was, would not go away. I was possessed by an evil spirit and in need of an exorcism. The torment I felt was so severe but nobody knew why. The nurses joined with Marisa to help calm me but to no avail. Nothing I had ever experienced before had prepared me for this. It was such a debilitating, piercing pain of unbelievable intensity. The pain was indescribable. When it struck I thought I was going to die. No one could help. 'The Team' seemed baffled. They carried out numerous tests, scans, X-rays, urine and blood samples and swab analysis. They took two sets of blood cultures which involved a doctor taking a small quantity of my blood and putting it into special bottles containing glucose broth that allows bacteria to grow. They then hoped to grow an organism that they could later identify and subsequently treat it.

That night a new 'Team' arrived to examine my joints. They informed me that my knees were full of liquid and needed to be drained.

'This is not a particularly painful procedure but at the same time not very pleasant.'

'Anything rarely is in a hospital,' I hissed.

'The technique is called an aspiration,' their leader continued, ignoring my tone, 'which is the removal of fluid using an instrument called an aspirator. An aspirator is a needle which uses suction to take the fluid out of a joint to relieve the swelling and examine the fluid.'

'Basically you're going to stick a big needle in my knees.'

'Yes, but you will feel better after it.'

I lay back and closed my eyes in an attempt to ignore what was happening. They took about fifteen minutes to finish both knees and then set about examining my ankles but, thankfully, they left them for another day.

It was difficult to get any decent amount of sleep because the pains sometimes struck during the day and sometimes very late at night. I felt vulnerable and shattered because of the lack of sleep, the trauma of the pains and the effects that the morphine and the antibiotics were having.

My body had by now taken on a strange appearance, so much so that we decided to take some photographs of it for posterity in case no one believed us in years to come. A look in the mirror revealed a dramatic transformation from the young red-haired athlete I was, to a grotesque, battered gaunt figure. There was nothing aerodynamic or athletic-looking left. My face had deep black lines of tiredness etched into it and I had aged years. I had turned into one of Mary Shelley's characters.

My joints were inflamed and my stomach bloated from the steroids; my body was covered in terrible bruises and I joked that Marisa had hit me with a big stick. The fact that I was bald and had lost over two stones in weight added to the overall effect. There was no denying that an encounter with me on a dark night would scare the living daylights out of many a person. I looked like a man I once met on a dark train in Transylvania who had burst into my compartment scantily clad and brandishing a glass bottle. Luckily he was so deranged that he didn't even notice my quick departure from the room.

Much to my relief, I stabilised a little the following week and Marisa booked a flight to go to Spain for two weeks. It was always an emotional time when she left, but I fully appreciated what an amazing job she was doing. I shuddered to think what I would have done without her. I wondered if the roles had been reversed if I could have lived in that room and slept on a mattress on the floor for months and months on end like that. It was such an unnatural life living in a hospital, yet she was amazing the way she handled it. To have companionship for those dreadful days on the ward was a luxury afforded to few patients.

Ciarán and Sandra, Madge and the others all kept an eye on me. However, my honeymoon from the attacks did not last long. Marisa had been gone only a few days when I got a fever and my temperature gradually rose to 40. Then the real nightmare began!

Just when I thought life was improving, it happened! The dreadful pains returned, except that this time they were much worse. Now the ferocious stinging blast was in my head!

As with the previous attacks in my joints, I had

a slight warning when the throbbing began, and I called for the nurses to get some morphine ready. Once more I was subjected to the terribly depressing routine of X-rays and scans, examinations, questions and, at times, patronising medics. Caroline and Barbara stayed with me at night. Pedro and Junior came at all hours of the day and night to ferry my possessed and afflicted body for more scans and tests. Corridors sprang up from everywhere as 'Dungeons and Dragons', came to mind.

With each spasm a light died within me. I could see no future and each breath was a struggle. I was so tired and distressed that I cried my eyes dry in agony. Hour after hour, wave after wave without respite. Elaine and Margaret were in and out of the room like a pair of honeybees trying to comfort me, but it was futile.

The pain took my breath away so much so that I could not bear to let go and breathe again. My temperature raged on and did not improve despite being hooked up to 'Drippy' twenty-four hours a day and having gallons of fluids and drugs pumped into me. In my wildest dreams I could never have imagined being so afflicted and distressed. Wave after wave of painful attacks debilitated me to such a degree that I lay rooted to the bed, drawn and exhausted.

Subsequent doses of morphine added to my weakened state and I just lay in the bed, corpse-like, praying to be saved from the torment. It took pain and suffering to another level. At times I was not sure if I would survive even to the end of the day. All my strength had vanished and, lethargic and listless, I dozed in a permanently horizontal position.

Marisa called at least twice a day, along with my family in Ireland. In the end Marisa returned from Spain. Instinctively she knew that I needed her. Along with the high fever and the terrible headaches came the vomiting. I cried, vomited and suffered agony and affliction.

Finally, after uncountable days of suffering, our prayers were answered when the problem was solved by simply giving me paracetamol every four hours. This lowered my temperature and prevented the headaches and vomiting. Slowly with each passing day the joint attacks abated and my problems faded as quickly as they had come.

A new doctor called Daniel, who was from Tasmania, Australia, arrived to take over from Demetri as head of 'The Team'. It was a natural progression as hospital personnel constantly changed, except, of course, for Marisa and me who were the only permanent fixtures at Barts! Daniel was of medium build, stocky, with brown hair and spoke in a pleasant soft voice. Immediately I felt at ease with him. He came to see me one day.

'I thought I'd come and have a chat. Your Hickman Line had been in since the start of May. It is standard practice to remove the Hickman Line when dealing with a persistent high temperature and with a line that has been in for quite a while. Some lines last longer and others a lot less, so you have been lucky there.'

'Oh, thanks, I didn't know I had any luck left. This could be the start of a beautiful relationship.'

'You're having a very rough time,' laughed

Daniel, 'but I promise I'll have you out of here in time for Christmas.'

'That is still four months away but I'll hold you to that promise.'

'Now, the removal of the line is done under local anaesthetic and it means that once it is gone, any drugs that need to be given will be done through a cannula.'

'That is not a pleasant thought. Cannulae are painful and awkward and usually last only a few days. You are the bearer of good news, Daniel,' I kidded.

The morning that they came to take out the line, I was unusually nervous. It must have been the combination of the fever and the anaesthetic, but for a few minutes I panicked, fearing that I might be operated on while still awake. I thought I could feel the terrible pain of a scalpel. I could hear voices and feel them pulling on my chest. It was a nightmare sensation but eventually the drugs worked and I dozed in my bed fitfully.

When I awoke I found the area heavily bandaged and my chest bruised and sore. Tired and in some discomfort from the week's exertions, I wanted to be left alone and given time to recover. Murphy's Law about 'anything that can go wrong will' was unfortunately proving to be all too accurate, with one setback following on another.

The doctors expected my temperature to stabilise and to slowly return to normal and for me to enjoy a period of rest and recuperation. Nothing could have been further from the truth! I was quickly finding out that logic did not apply when dealing with cancer, and a combination of the past few months seemed to have finally caught up with me.

By the third week of September I had regressed significantly. We had been back on the ward with the joint and head problem for some twenty-five days when it took effect. It was not that anything dramatic suddenly happened but just the way that my daily life was changed. Now the days and nights, weeks and weekends synthesised into one and the same. It all merged to such a degree that I no longer noticed the difference any more.

Time was not important and had lost its significance and I floated from moment to moment, lost in my own little world, conscious yet unable to do anything about my plight. At one stage we counted every hour of every day to see when I could leave the hospital, but now I did not even think about it. In the past I would question any of the medics and nurses about the drugs and my condition, but not anymore.

It was all in the distant past and I no longer cared, even when they stuck needles in me. They went unheeded and were insignificant and unimportant. My movements became limited in the extreme and at times I had to be forced out of my bed so the sheets could be changed and the room cleaned. Sometimes I did not even have the energy to sit in a chair or to go to the toilet or to wash.

Lethargic and depressed, I constantly thought about my family in Ireland and how much I wanted to be with them. This desire to lead a normal life was also reflected in the fact that I wanted to go out with Marisa and have fun just like other couples, but being in a hospital for so long was so unnatural and rendered it impossible. Because of my immune system and general ill health, at times we could not even kiss or hold hands. Everything was such a struggle; my lack of energy was as worrying as my dearth of drive and desire.

I had no interest in anything, no motivation or enthusiasm. Reading the paper was a problem because my hands were so shaky that I found it hard to concentrate for any length of time. Writing was definitely out and the television made me melancholy and sad. I found some degree of comfort in cartoons or animated movies. Marisa put on a video I had about the great milers which inspired me for a time, but eventually I lost concentration and drifted off.

We still had plenty of callers and visitors to keep us busy. However, the number of people allowed at any one time was strictly regulated. Because of my poor state, anyone who wanted to visit us was advised to ring first to check with the nurses or Marisa to see if it was okay for them to visit. Anyone with a cold or virus could not come near me because of my poor condition. Deprived of strength and energy, I struggled in the company of others. My concentration was so poor at times that despite wanting to talk and let them know that I appreciated their efforts, frequently I slept throughout their visits.

One morning, when 'The Team' came on their rounds, I told them that I had sweated a lot during the night and felt terrible. They booked some X-rays to check a few things out. I knew they would send the 'T Rex' to me. It was a great machine because they could bring it onto the ward and into the room of very sick people to take X-rays. I called it that because of its long neck, which reminded me of one of 'The Raptors' or the 'Tyrannosaurus Rex' in Jurassic Park.

That night I was sweating yet again and after a visit to the toilet noticed blood in my faeces. Later I had a coughing attack and spat some phlegm out into the sink. Marisa noticed that there was also blood in it, which must have come from my chest. We buzzed the nurses immediately and soon the doctors were on the scene to signal the start of another crisis.

At once I was subjected to more scans and X-rays, more samples of faeces, urine, blood and blood cultures. The nurses came hourly to check my readings and monitor my health. A galaxy of drips and tubes went up and I was pumped full of blood, platelets, fluids and antibiotics. In one continuous cycle, blood went in one end and out the other.

Understandably, I was rocked at this latest problem and very disappointed. The events that followed the discovery of the blood then took a very strange twist. Although it did not seem possible, I shifted down several gears, wilting visibly with each passing day. The bed was now my only place of residence, and from the supine everything moved around me in slow motion. At times I was aware of what was happening, but mostly I was an onlooker, physically present but not a participant.

My overall health deteriorated and the amount of attention I received increased considerably. They stuck more needles in me than any self-respecting pincushion and gave me fluids and tablets by the ton. I, of course, had no say in any of it. I was so weary that it seemed that my very life was being sucked out of me. My body and mind felt incapable of rallying and despite my eternal promise, when I first became ill in 1993 that I would never give up, I now felt very close to it. I was on the edge.

One day I opened my eyes and Marisa was crying.

'What's wrong, love?'

'Nothing. I'll be fine. How are you feeling?'

'Shattered.'

'You are going to get better. Be strong.'

'I hope I get better soon,' I wheezed with difficulty.

Daniel and another doctor called Jonathan came into the room. He was a thin man with black glasses and of average height. We had never spoken but I had seen him many times before as part of 'The Team'.

'We are starting you on some new injections. These injections are designed especially to help boost your white cells and therefore will help fight the infection,' said Jonathan.

'Don't tempt fate. It's me we are talking about. Have you any drugs left in the cabinet that I have not had?' There was a brief silence, then Daniel spoke.

'Because your immune system is so weak and depressed, we believe that you have a kind of septicaemia. This means that bacteria with a very long name is in your blood stream causing problems. We will continue with the antibiotics and we will now introduce conventional tuberculosis treatment.'

'Tuberculosis!'

I tried to talk to them but my eyes would not stay open. Marisa helped me put on the oxygen mask. She was stroking my face. It felt nice and I started to drift. Jimi Hendrix visited my dreams and my mind was clouded full of purple haze.

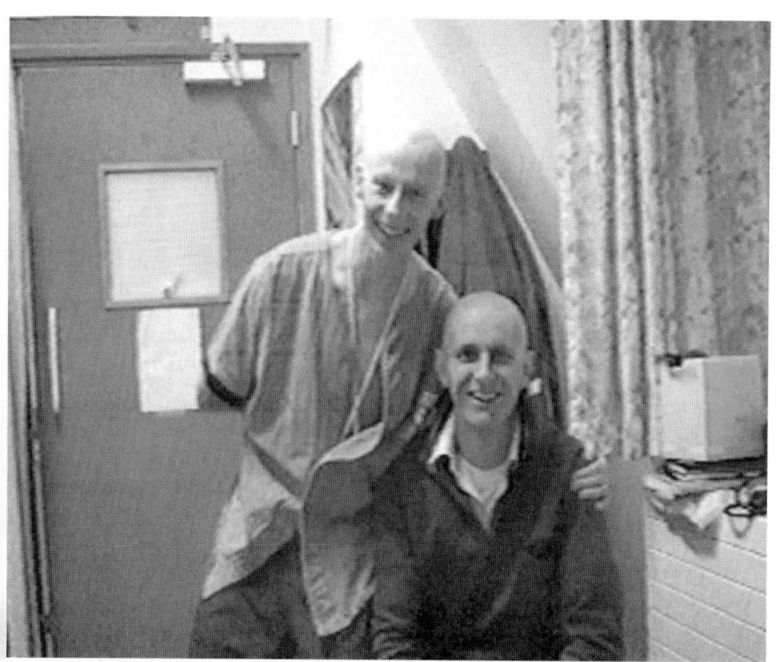
The cone heads. Me and Ivan Hargreaves in my room at Barts. 1994

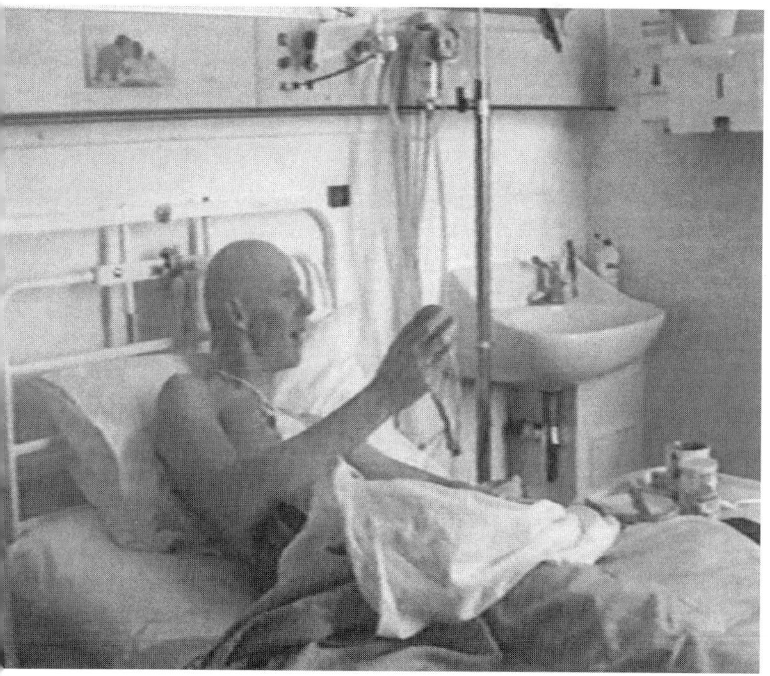
Relaxing in my hospital bed while attached to ‘Drippy’. Barts. 1994

Celebrating Marisa's bitrhday in our room at St Barts

Playing with my Hickman Line while singing a tune

In our rom during the 1994 World Cup. At least I can blame the drugs

With Marisa and Mam at the fountain in St Bartholomew's Hospital

Me, Jamie, Lar, Pat, Tom

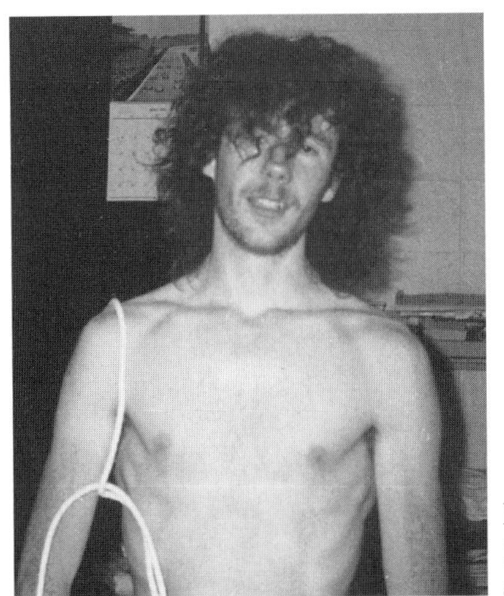

Me in Tennesse
1984. A Hendri
child

Tara, Mam,
Aisling and
Simon with
baby Sean.
1997

The lads. Dermot, Tom, Jamie, Domo and Me. 1998

Marisa toasting to the future

The mad McClary clan.
Catherine, Madge, Ian

Enjoying life in Roundwood. Sean, Ruth, Mam, Me and John

A Fiesta in Melilla. Margarita, Celia and me. 1997

Celebrating our birthdays. At the back, Anne and myself
In front Margarita, Marisa, Michelle and John

Marisa and me at the Love Lounge having won a trip to New York for Valentine's weekend 1998

Dad, Ruth, Dermot and Norah at Dad's sixty nineth birthday

Mam, me and Ruth 1999

Marisa and Margarita

A feast at the Leacys. Anne, Aidan, Me, Aidan & James

Our philosophy for the future. Seize the moment and never give in. Party on. Right. Growing together. John and me. 1999. Below. Marisa, Dino, Madge and me. July 2000

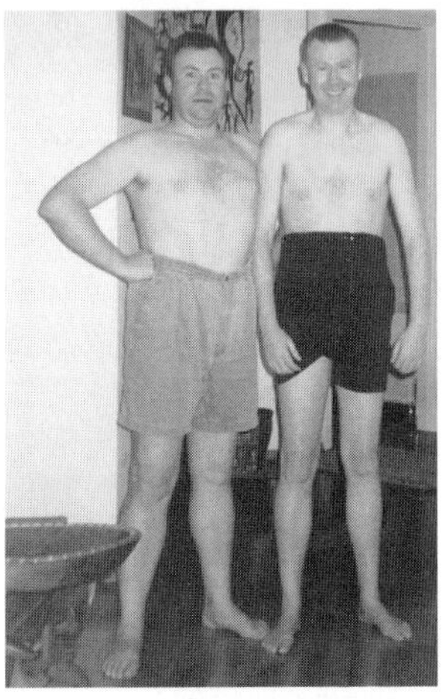

A surprise party for my 36th birthday. July 2000

13

LOST IN SPACE

When I was nine, I used to buy the Marvel Comics in a shop in Blackrock village. One of the characters was called Doctor Strange. He was able to leave his body and float out of it to see things in different time dimensions and places. The cocktail of drugs led my mind a merry dance. Right then lying in such an ill state with a raging fever and burning disease in my body, I felt exactly like Dr Strange.

It was a terrible yet at the same time fascinating experience. Suddenly I was transported back in dreams and nightmares, only to awaken confused and disorientated. It was like the start of the Terminator movies, where they arrive from the future in a lightning storm and, dazed and confused, ask 'What month is it? What year is it?'

As I lay there semiconscious, on the edge, my mind relived my life and sometimes my darker side, asking why I had done this and why I had failed at that, questioning decisions I had made and searching for answers to unanswerable questions. Sometimes I was aware of precisely what was happening but at others times I was lost somewhere in a world of hallucinations, dreams, flashbacks and nightmares. They whizzed about with no respect or regard for time or order.

My mind floated back to America 1984. I was in the back of a car reading passages from *'On the Road'* by Jack Kerouac. I was driving to New York with two friends: Gary, who was from Long Island, and Ross from North Dakota. I felt like a real dude, a low rider, heading off with my buddies on my first road trip, playing tunes, cruising along without a care in the world.

The next day Gary and his younger brother Jimmy took us into Manhattan to show us the sights. It was one of the biggest shopping days of the year and we went all over Manhattan visiting the sites. Time did not matter in this city as we traversed it until the early hours of the morning. In Times Square two of the lads jumped the barriers without paying.

I was last through and as I walked away, I heard some shouting but thought nothing of it and ran to catch up with the others. I jumped on Gary's back and we tumbled to the ground laughing. Then someone stuck a gun in my face.

'Get up,' a rough voice shouted. I looked up to see about ten or twelve police surrounding us, guns drawn.

I was dragged up, thrown up against the wall, legs and arms spread-eagled. Shit! Fare evasion is serious business here I thought. A dozen questions were fired at us from all angles. I was amazed at all the aggression, so confrontational! Dirty Harry was ringing clear in my head.

After about twenty minutes they finally

released us. They fined me for disturbing the peace and as we were leaving I turned to one of them and asked, 'What happened anyway, who did you think we were?'

'Murderers,' he casually replied.

'What?'

'That's right, smart ass,' he continued 'you almost got your head blown off running away from the police like that.'

I was speechless. It turned out that a gang had just murdered someone in the station right beside where we were seen jumping the barriers and running off. Needless to say, his reply shocked me. Wow, what a country!

Now I moved on to two years later.

I had been racing in Oklahoma City at the American Championships and as half term began, I decided to go back to Tennessee to visit my old college friends. A mix-up in arrangements left me stranded in Oklahoma without a lift until I secured one from the Arkansas track team whose coach and some athletes were Irish. My delight at securing a ride to their university in Fayetteville soon turned to despair as it was just inside the Arkansas border.

Four hours later I was deposited in the middle of the town and pointed in the direction of the bus station. Disappointed that I had not received more help from some of my fellow Irish compatriots, I set off dejected. I had not been walking long when a police car pulled alongside me. Inside the car sat a short, fat, sweaty, red-faced sheriff wearing sunglasses and chewing tobacco. He immediately reminded me of Sheriff J. W. Pepper from the Bond movie 'Live and Let Die'. I looked somewhat amused at him and he stuck his head out the window, spat on the ground and proclaimed 'Boy, you look like a runaway.' I was very tired, in a bad mood, and probably lost. Not only that but the sheriff from 'Dweebcounty Arkansas' star of the 'First Blood' and the 'Rambo movies' was hard on my heels. It was the last thing I needed.

'Well if I am, I've run a very long way.'

'What's that you say boy?'

'I'm lost, looking for the bus station.' I replied still walking.

'You're not from round here then.'

I could feel his eyes burning up and down me especially my wild shoulder-length flaming red hair. Granted I looked a bit of a mess, being tired from the physical demands of the weekend's racing and the hassles of trying to get to Tennessee. However the last thing I needed was some fat redneck policeman harassing me.

'Where are you from, boy?' he drawled and then spat again from a huge wad of tobacco stuffed in his fat left cheek. It was obvious he disliked me.

'Ireland,' I said in a thick Dublin accent, knowing he would not have a clue what I said.

'What?'

'Ireland,' I repeated, giving him the old only an idiot would not know what I said look.

'What island?' he asked, irritated.

'Not an island, Ireland!' I said, just as irritated.

'Damn boy,' he rasped. 'What kind of weird accent you got?'

'I told you, I'm from Ireland. You know it's a country, in Europe, beside England, capital city Dublin!'

'Damn, don't you speak no English? Move ya ass over there.'

So there he was 'Old Top Dog Sheriff Bubba No Brains' from 'Dweeb County' doing his duty and harassing me. Important Stuff!

'Got some identification then, boy?'

'Sure,' I said putting down my bags.

'Don't make any sudden moves now, I'm watching.' It was a stupid situation but I had no choice and handed him my student card and driving licence.

'Idaho, damn you have come a long way. What are you, a drifter?' He went back to his car and called in the information over the radio and I sat down. After about ten minutes he waddled back.

'Looks like you're okay. You're a foreigner and a track star. Checked your college records,' he rasped with his thick southern drawl and spat on the ground.

'I told you I'm from Dublin, Ireland, studying in Idaho.'

'Damn boy, I thought you meant Dublin, Pennsylvania. You Australian or something?'

'Irish, you know, Leprechauns and shamrocks, and Guinness.'

'Yeah, hot damn I got you now, that's the place with all the fighting going on. That's how come you run so fast, running away from them tanks and bullets chasing you!' Then he unleashed another huge spit from his gob and laughed.

'Nasty habit you got there. You could get cancer. Anyway I never saw a gun in my life until now, or in some Western or war movie about Vietnam.'

He visibly winced at that and I wished I'd had a wad of tobacco to spit vehemently. He handed me back my cards.

'Is that why America took you in then? Like them boat people. Come here and learn English.'

'No,' I said incredulously. 'I am here because I am a damn good athlete. They pay for my degree and I win races.' He starred at me, spat again, then walked back to his car. I gathered my bags. Our meeting was finished. He started the engine.

'The bus station is two miles straight ahead. I'm going that way but I've got some important business to take care of first.' He grinned.

'Oh that's okay' I said, 'I enjoy walking. I don't want to get fat now do I?' With that I grinned and headed off. Important business my ass, but at least now you know where the hell Ireland is! He swung the car round and took off towards the bus station. And that was that. Praise the Lord. Amen.

My body floated on again. I was now sitting at my desk writing in my diary.

Diary: 30 June 1992. My rooms at St. Edmund's.

Travelling around Europe at Easter has helped lift the gloom and made me realise that I have to take time out to sort out my life and what I really want from it. I know that I am at a real crossroads. My running has deteriorated so much that I now realise that I cannot possibly compete at a decent level this year. It is a shocking truth but I know that to be a top class athlete one has to have all the many different component parts in order and if, for example, one's mental approach is not right then that affects everything else. My confidence is low after all the poor races and the imminent divorce. It is obvious that I am physically and emotionally simply not in the right shape or frame of mind to race. It really hurts me inside to be struggling in races and training knowing that I used to be able to do it so easily. I no longer enjoy it. What is wrong with me? I have the talent but in this environment I am only fooling myself to think that I can keep up the same level of commitment to that of my American days. As the summer holidays approach, I am abandoning all thoughts of competing competitively on the track. I need to get away from everything and everyone. I am so depressed and disheartened that this is the only way that I can solve my problems.

This trip will be a huge landmark in my life as it will be the first time since I was about ten years old that I will not be spending the summer months racing on an athletics track. Broken-hearted at my meteoric fall. I am sad and alone. I am no longer an athlete. I hope to rise from the ashes like the phoenix.

My body floated on to one month later.

July 1992, San Fermin, Pamplona, northern Spain.

Jesus Maria Blanco was a friend at St Edmund's who had come from Spain to improve his English for a year. He lived in Pamplona, home of the San Fermin. Every year from the 7 to 14 of July the San

Fermin Festival attracted hundreds of thousands of people for a religious festival, and more famously for the running of the bulls. My friendship with Jesus whetted my appetite sufficiently to lure me halfway across Europe from Romania through Austria where I met Roger Gall and down into Spain. Never could I have believed that on 12 July 1992 I would be standing in that same town contemplating such a crazy idea.

On my arrival in Pamplona I was shocked by the sheer volume of people on the streets. Thousands meandered in all directions. People flowed down the streets like plagues of jungle ants sweeping all before them. I grabbed a taxi to avoid the crazy scenes and headed to Jesus's house. I knew that Jesus would not be there for a week but his family welcomed me with open arms. His younger sister Inma knew some English and through her I managed to communicate with her Mum, Dad and brother, Roberto. That night I watched television coverage of the bull run and read newspaper clippings from the past few days which left me in no doubt that this was a very dangerous event. For the first time I began to reconsider my quest for adventure and bravado.

Later Inma and her friend Itzir took me out to sample the atmosphere of the San Fermin. The Fiesta exploded before my eyes in an amazing displaying of colour, noise, music and energy. Never before or since have I experienced such a phenomenon. The square was solid with people dancing, drinking and singing. We could hardly breathe in the crowd, let alone move. Everyone operated at a snail's pace.

Drums pounded and bands played. There was no room to dance but everyone tried as even more people flooded into the squares from the side streets. All I could see were heads bobbing up and down in one massive Pogo. We held hands to make a chain as we snaked our way through the masses. The display was amazing as it lit up the clear sky. I was intoxicated with the rhythms, the sounds and the colours of the fiesta and the local wine. It was great to be alive. I wanted the moment to last forever.

'Buenos días ven a comer. Toma esto, para la fiesta.' Opening my eyes I saw Jesus's mother calling me for some breakfast. It was seven in the morning but I thought that I had just got into bed. She presented me with a red scarf to wear in the run. Embarrassed, I took it and bravely pronounced, 'Hasta la vista, gracias.'

Decked out in my runners, cut off jeans, a white tee shirt and my red scarf, I headed off for the town centre. A river of bodies moved along the streets and finally I reached the wooden barriers. Thousands of people jostled for position to get the best view of the run.

Between the barricades, on both sides of the cobbled streets, runners waited nervously for the start. No one was in control as the tide of bodies swayed with the flow. It was now or never. I took one last deep breath and climbed under the barricade into danger. I had finally rediscovered the old adrenaline rush from my athletic days. Everybody was nervous, pushing and singing and jumping. The noise was deafening yet intoxicating and my muscles cried out for release. I felt alive and ready to go.

A huge roar went up as the final minutes

ticked by and Pamplona prepared to celebrate another historic Bull Run. The crowd started to push forward as the first signs of nerves surfaced. Everyone was singing, both on the ground and in the balconies overlooking the run. People threw water down on the crowd to cool them from the heat as some began walking towards the finish. Voices rose into the sky and emotional fervour gripped me.

Back at the start of the run, the runners gathered at the statue of San Fermin to sing one last song. On the stroke of eight the rocket was lit and blasted into the sky. The gates suddenly flew open and unleashed the twelve animals onto the streets. There were some cows in there to lead the bulls along, yet they too were more than capable of causing serious damage.

Suddenly I was flung forward like a shot from a cannon and was impaled against a barricade, scraping my arm badly. Pandemonium broke out and someone started hitting me.

'Venga tu, corre corre, corre rápido,' screamed a man above me on the barricade. 'Venga, run!'

Gathering my wits, I pushed off into the mayhem and started to run. Almost immediately, I nearly fell over a woman who had fallen in front of me. A few people with noble but futile intentions tried to stop and pick her up but were themselves bowled over by the onrushing crowd. A drunk crashed head first into the wooden panels and fell, bleeding heavily.

I heard a big shout and a scream as the bulls arrived in force. Three brutes rounded the bend just feet from where I desperately sought to avoid another pile up. They disposed of runners with ease and continued towards the tunnel. Within seconds I approached the stadium with the statue of Hemingway at its entrance. Ernest, my man, you have a lot to answer for I thought as I began my descent into the tunnel.

'Toros, toros' people screamed.

Bodies littered the narrow tunnel and I ran, fighting my way over a massive pile up. I smashed my knee into the side of someone's head as people fell; they tried to get up only to be knocked down again by the onslaught. I glanced over my shoulder and was horrified to spot a black bull crashing into the wooden side. Two more animals tripped as well and dragged down a dozen people with them. The pain in my knee went instantly with thoughts of the bulls goring and crushing all behind me.

I pushed forward until I reached the sandy ground of the stadium. People spilled out of the tunnel into the stadium where the populace of thirty thousand was going crazy, shouting and screaming encouragement to the runners. The low walls of the bullring drew me like a magnet and I shot over them to sanctuary.

'Yeeehooo!' I screamed with all my might. People celebrated and hugged complete strangers and the fiesta began. I sat with my head on my knees nursing my bruises. A big crowd stayed inside the ring even when all the bulls had been taken out through the main gates. There were some announcements in Spanish and then I noticed a group sitting on the sand only fifteen yards from the main gates. They sat in two lines parallel to each other, leaving a gap of about ten feet between the groups.

Then! The gates flew open and like a rocket a

bull charged out, flashing between the sitting groups. Round and round the ring the bull went. Seconds later a second bull entered the ring to cause more chaos. People were knocked over the barriers and dispatched with ease, especially the drunks. They knocked unsuspecting revellers sky high. People started chasing the bulls, trying to touch them as the careered around the dirt. The whole spectacle lasted about twenty minutes. Bulls chasing people and people chasing bulls. It was a crazy end to a crazy day.

'Hola Mark, qué tal?'

'Hola, amigo,' I replied, as I recognised Itzir's father from the night before.

He invited me to have some churros, a typical breakfast taken with hot chocolate. Neither of us could speak the other's language, but we went into a tiny crowded bar full of runners and people, some singing, some drinking. He clasped me in a vice-like grip, obviously delighted to see me. I could not understand anything he told me but I grinned from ear to ear, happy to see him and happy to be alive.

That night Paul Harnett, an Australian friend who was working at St Edmund's, arrived, and I relived the whole experience again the next day. Two fantastic weeks later I left Pamplona, having run twice, celebrated my birthday, tasted alcohol for the first time and spent a memorable time with Jesus, Roberto and their family. It was the most exciting holiday experience I had ever had and I vowed to return some day when I could speak Spanish.

14

LIVING ON THE EDGE

I opened my eyes to see Marisa and Elaine looking over me.

'I need to take some observations,' Elaine said gently. 'You are sweating and moving around a lot and I was afraid you would pull the cannula out of your arm.'

'Lots of dreams and nightmares and I feel spaced out. How long have I been sleeping?'

'Hardly at all,' replied Marisa. 'I just went to the kitchen to make some tea and I was talking to the nurses.'

'I've lost track of everything, especially the time.'

'Don't worry, Mark,' said Elaine, 'I will go and get my gloves and a bag to change your sheets because of the risk of contamination.'

'Mark's hands are very shaky,' said Marisa.

'That's because his potassium level is so low but it will eventually improve.'

'The potassium drinks are disgusting and the tablets are like golf balls. I don't know what to do.'

Someone helped me put the oxygen mask on. A strap went over my head, the mask went over my face and the two little tubes went inside my nostrils. I found it uncomfortable but I had to use it regularly to help me breathe. I slept a little and awoke to see Father Peter by my bed. Marisa and Elaine were not in the room. Father Peter had a pleasant reassuring manner.

'I just popped in to see how you were.'

'I'm constantly waking and sleeping.'

'Would you like some communion and to say a prayer?'

'I don't know if I can stay awake.'

Father Peter smiled kindly and took out his Bible and a little box or packet of some sort. My eyes kept closing and I could not focus properly. I fought to keep awake but I was so very tired. The communion touched my mouth and I heard Marisa's voice. She gave me a sip of water and then my eyes closed. Later 'The Team' arrived. I saw shapes rather than people and they swarmed all over me. Mam and Dad rang and 'The Team' left. Marisa spoke to my parents as I was too weak and they said they were coming to visit me.

'You are a fighter, aren't you?' Marisa asked.

'We all are really.'

'But you have to keep fighting for me and never stop.'

'I don't want to die. It's just that it gets so hard at times. I hope I don't die.'

'You won't if you believe you're going to get better. Promise me you will keep fighting.'

'Yes I promise.'

'We both need to be strong. You have done so well. Please keep fighting and be strong.'

Tears filled our eyes and we hugged each other and cried together in private. Probably for the first time ever, I knew I was critically ill and it was a strange realisation. They kept giving me oxygen every few hours and I thought I looked like a fighter pilot from 'Star Wars' with the mask on. Daniel was in and out of the door many times and life ticked slowly by like the ebb and flow of a tide on a sandy beach. My head was so mixed up. Then I was sick. It happened so quickly that I could not help it. Feebly I looked up to see Marisa smiling at me. Of course, Marisa was there looking after me. My eyes closed since they were too heavy to keep open. I could hear noises and voices in the room, yet my eyes would not respond and open. I had no idea where I was. At times I thought I was dead, in hell or was it purgatory? I did not know whether I even existed anymore.

Then at some stage later I was aware of Marisa sitting in her chair.

'Some doctors came by to see you but said they would be back later. Kirsty came to say that they will send 'T Rex' to take some X-rays.'

'Thanks love, you're a great secretary.'

My bottom and back were really sore from being in the bed so much. I was hooked up for more fluids and a blood transfusion and my movements were restricted for fear of pulling the cannula out or knocking over 'Drippy'.

DREAM

1. mental activity usually an imagined series of events occurring during sleep.

2. a sequence of imaginative thoughts indulged in while awake.

3. aspiration.
4. a vain hope.

Was I dreaming? My brain was working slowly, trying to get a grip on everything that was happening. I told my body to fight, to work at it just like in a race. Pretend it's a race I demanded, you used to be good at that. Somebody lifted my head and gave me a drink of water. My mouth was incredibly dry and it was such a relief to feel some moist liquid in it even though it was difficult to swallow. Sipping the water vaguely reminded me of the dream I had just had; but then I forgot it just as quickly. Images and memories invaded my mind without warning. Bombarding my weakened body with rhymes and bits of learning from school days; little insignificant moments from my life; recollections of former races; the lads playing football; rugby matches and teachers from school. It was a roller coaster of highs and lows which left me emotionally distraught. I was losing my mind, babbling incoherently, the walls were closing in on me, I was hallucinating and fading into the bed, through the floor, down to the psychiatric ward.

"Letters to the walls of silence"

Knowledge begins with thee
from without you cannot see
spiders flies and footpaws too
not alone just me and you
ages pass and your still there
never barren never bare

but what good in the end
no cry no comment to recommend
just an empty silence

Michele and Jackie came from St Edmund's to visit. We talked a little but I was feeling out of it. They talked about the holy bone of Saint Edmund and about helping me and then they left. My bedsores were multiplying and there was talk of getting me a special mattress. In order to relieve some of the pain and discomfort, I sat on three pillows. Daniel arrived and left the room with Marisa. Voices coming and going, in and out of the room and in my head. Visions and effigies, horrible and wild. Apocalypse Now. Napalm strikes. A voice nagged away in my head talking to me. Was it a devil or an angel? My mind was terribly confused and disorientated.

'TIME IS ALL THE SAME NOW, ISN'T IT MARK?'

'WHO ARE YOU?'

'I'M YOU. I AM YOUR SPIRIT SOUL.'

'WHY ARE YOU HERE?'

'TO HELP YOU THROUGH THE LAST BIT. YOUR CLOCK IS RUNNING.'

'WHAT'S HAPPENING TO ME?'

'YOU'RE FADING. WE GOT A MESSAGE THAT YOU ARE READY.'

'READY FOR WHAT?'

'TO LEAVE. TO SAY ADIOS. IT'S OVER.'

'AM I DEAD? I DON'T WANT...'

I awoke with a jolt. It was probably 'The Terminators' but something woke me up. I could not see anyone. Was I back travelling through

Romania again? Just like the time I awoke on the train on my way to Dracula's Castle in Transylvania. Even though the carriage was pitch dark, I knew somebody was standing beside me. It's the morphine, you eegit. No there he is! A huge man, bald, cuts all over his body, no shoes or clothes on except a potato sack around his groin. He is going to kill me. Oh Jesus! No! Please no!

Marisa came to the bed and wet my brow and gave me a sip of water. My mouth was like sandpaper. It felt as if I had walked in the Sahara for months. I tried to speak but I did not know if I was making any sound?

'Relax, Mark. I think you were having a nightmare. Your temperature is racing but the fluids are going in slowly. Nicola has just gone off duty. She has been in a few times to check on you. I am going to lie down for a while but I'll be here if you need me.'

'I do not want to die. Please don't leave.'

'You won't, love. You're great. I'm right here.'

'I love you,' I mumbled.

Sleep came and went as it pleased. I constantly shifted in the bed, moaning and groaning as I tried to get comfortable. I had no idea where I was or what time of the day, month or year it was. There was a time when the day had had clearly defined periods from breakfast through to the evening, but not now. Somebody moved me and then I felt the sting of a needle in my stomach. I wanted to cry out in pain but I couldn't and just whimpered in defeat.

I awoke to see Father Pinot, from St Edmund's, talking to Marisa. He was the priest and maths teacher at the school. He had a little box with him and was in the middle of saying some prayers. To the best of my ability I joined in but then drifted off. Time went by and a blend of hospital lights and my illness rendered my sense of time and space completely useless. Someone gently moved me.

'Son. Mark can you hear me?'

'Dad! How long have you been here?'

'Not long, Mark,' he answered as he kissed my forehead.

My mother held my hands and kissed my cheeks. Her eyes were red from crying and I was very sad to see her suffering so much. Ruth and John came into the room with Marisa and there were hugs and kisses all round. I was so happy to see them all that I cried. Marisa brought a tray with tea and biscuits for them and, for a few brief moments my life was whole again having my loved ones with me. A knock on the door woke me up and dozens of doctors arrived in. 'The Team' crammed into the room, talked for a while and were gone again.

Later Father Peter came to visit. He talked and prayed with my family. Everybody was there again huddled around my bed, deep in prayer. A hand touched my forehead and I opened my eyes to see him leaning over me, then slowly they closed and darkness descended on me. I slept with the voices in my head.

'SAIGON. SHIT I'M IN THE JUNGLE...'

'YOU FAILED. LOSER. YOU NEVER RAN IN THE...'

'MARK. PATIENT 120...NO PLATELETS. PAIN.'

'GUILTY OF... GONE FOREVER.'

'STOP IT! BE POSITIVE! FIGHT BACK. DON'T GIVE UP.

'WHO IS THAT?'

'ARE YOU GOING TO MAKE UP YOUR MIND?'

'WHAT DO YOU MEAN?'

'NOW I HEAR YOU DON'T WANT TO COME.'

'I'M VERY TIRED.'

'THEN HURRY UP AND LET GO. MY SIGNAL IS GETTING WEAKER, SO YOU MUST DECIDE.'

'DECIDE WHAT?'

'LOOK, IT'S SIMPLE. JUST ASK YOURSELF ONE QUESTION. ARE YOU GOING TO DIE OR GOING TO GET BETTER?'

'I WANT TO LIVE.'

'GREAT. SO IF YOU DON'T NEED ME NOW I'LL BE OFF.'

'WILL I SEE YOU AGAIN?'

'SURE. I AM YOU AND YOU ARE ME, OKAY. HASTA LA VISTA.'

My head was lifted and I received water. I felt the burn of a needle in my arm and groaned. The cannula was blocked and my wrist hurt terribly. Then I was rolled over on my side and my arms were lifted up. My body was pushed and pulled but I was on the periphery.

15

DELIVERANCE

My eyes adjusted to the room and its Christmas decorations and I knew I was back from trips down memory lane. It was all the morphine, the illness and the fatigue that led to so many dreams, memories and nightmares coming at me from all angles. Time passed and I drifted fitfully in my bed. I was exhausted but I felt slightly more aware of what was going on. My eyes scanned the room. Then I took in the state of my body and the drips attached to 'Drippy'. I knew that I was on the edge, not at all well, but at least I was still alive. Marisa came to the room and hugged me.

'Hi, love. You look a bit better. There's more colour in your face but you are sweating so much. Your pyjamas are soaking again. I'll go and tell the nurses.'

Marisa left the room and soon returned with Margaret who was carrying a pink plastic bag and wearing protective gloves.

'I have a clean pair of pyjamas ready,' said Marisa.

'There's the man of the moment,' announced Margaret. 'Worrying us all to bits. We thought we had lost you. We'll get you changed and you will be smelling of roses. It's also time for another stab.'

'There's a fellow Celt for you,' I complained weakly.

Marisa was in and out of the room as were one or two of the doctors. The nurses were changing shift, 'doing the hand over'. The clock showed 9.30 pm so I had been resting for two hours. It was all I ever did and I worried if I would ever regain my strength again? It was bright from the lights of the ward and I could hear the strange squeaky sounds of the building. Somebody up the corridor was groaning in pain. Poor bugger! The nurses' phone was ringing incessantly.

God, familiarity does breed contempt. It was nearly two years since I had first became ill and I was still in hospital and in need of its medical expertise. I knew Barts inside and out, better than most of the doctors and nurses because the personnel changed regularly but, me, the patient, I was still here. Yet of course the simple answer was to take one day at a time. I reminded myself just how far I had come and that I was still alive. That itself was a major achievement.

The Septicaemia was a very serious problem and the past thirty-six hours had been touch and go. I received the sacrament once from Father Peter and another time from Father Pinot, who had brought the bone of St Edmund to try to help me. Michele, Jackie and Madge had all talked to him, as the bone was believed to have miraculous healing powers following several cases where it had been successful in helping people to recover when all seemed to be lost. The fact that I had come through the critical few days was a good sign.

Marisa held my hand and my whole family came in to say hello. They were understandably relieved to see me awake and attentive. I received hugs from everyone in the room and was greeted by big beaming smiles. 'The Team' then came and reiterated the fact that it was a very close call and that I was still not out of the woods.

'The injections, TB tablets and the drips all need to continue,' began Daniel. 'You'll be on the tablets for nine months but gradually you will improve and regain your strength. The more you can avoid being horizontal, the quicker your respiratory system will recover.'

As I improved slowly, the drama which had unfolded was related to me. Marisa had informed my family that I had deteriorated a lot in one week and they all came over to London immediately. During the first week of October my life was on the line and it was touch and go. They even took blood tests from John in case a last ditch transplant was needed. While I lay in the bed degenerating rapidly, my loved ones lived from hour to hour anxiously awaiting signs of improvement and words of encouragement from the medics. Now, with every passing hour, my chances of surviving increased.

By the end of the following week, my family returned to Ireland, happy at least that the real danger had passed. I was sad to see them go but I looked forward to seeing them all again at Christmas.

'Where are your bracelet and rings?' I asked

Marisa one day, noticing that she had not worn them for a while.

'I removed all of them on the 5th. I was very upset and crying because I was so worried about you. That night I made a promise to God that if you lived I would not wear any jewellery or get my hair cut for a year.'

'Muchas gracias,' I replied and kissed her.

One morning after a titanic effort to get out of the bed, I stepped on the scales. To my horror the figures eight and a half stone, 54 kilos flashed at me. I had lost one and a half stone in 20 weeks! The demise in my weight was equalled only by my lack of energy. It was a terrific struggle even to get out of bed and to just sit in a chair in the room, but it was vital that I did so to give my lungs a chance to expand and to breathe properly.

Just as I had hated missing training as an athlete, I now realised that the longer I lay in the bed the worse off I would become. Any movement of my legs and body muscles, no matter how little, stimulated blood flow and got my heart pumping again. I knew only too well just how fast muscles atrophied, and I tried to stand a little bit every day. Even a few minutes moving around the room left me exhausted and at times I cried with frustration at my weak state. However it never lasted for a long time and psychologically I knew that it was very important to get out of the bed, and the room, if possible. I really tried not to allow a barrier to develop as happens with some people who become institutionalised and do not want to leave the hospital.

One day Daniel came to talk to me.

'I know it has been hard on you spending such a long time in this room and if you would like or think it might help, then I could arrange for a psychiatrist to have a chat with you.'

'There are days when I think I am going to crack up but when that happens I just imagine that I am out running on the trails in Idaho or in mountains in Wicklow, floating over the ground. I am aware of everything, spaced out and yet conscious of all that is around me. On other occasions I think back to training sessions when I was running at my peak. I would accelerate off the last bend and really feel that I was running fast, almost faster than my legs could turn over. It is a great feeling and it is what keeps me sane, especially at night when I cannot sleep and have so much time to reflect on life.'

'Well you certainly are strong but the facility is there if you would like to talk to someone.'

At first, Marisa brought me in a wheelchair down to the kitchen where I would meet staff and patients. These were vital moments designed to bring me out of my little cocoon. Mingling with other people again helped to stimulate my mind and encouraged me to keep fighting.

I continued to improve slowly and by the end of October, just three weeks after the priests had been to see me, I was strong enough to go for short walks around the ward. Weather permitting, we ventured down to the square in the afternoons and enjoyed the peace sitting beside the fountain. It was my favourite time of day, as I really felt that I was making progress when I was out in the fresh air.

The daily routine of tablets and transfusions continued, but for the first time in months I began to see light at the end of the tunnel. The pain in my joints had vanished and, even though I was still taking over sixty tablets a day, I felt I had turned the corner. I tried not to think about how close I had come to dying but there was no doubt that I was lucky to be still alive.

Another patient on the ward who had become a good friend of ours had sadly lost his fight and passed away. The day I was anointed with the bone of St Edmund, he arrived at my room to visit me. He was very ill as well but because of my own poor state of health I had no idea that he would die the next day, making it the fourth such loss I had known there. We had previously talked about our own situations and the different problems we faced. He always had a sense of resignation about his health and outlook on life, despite all the encouragement that we tried to give him. His loss reinforced how critical it was to never give up hope and that I must not let myself get so close again to doing just that. I had to always remain positive, no matter what.

As time marched on we heard that I would be allowed to leave on 9 November. All the hardship and adversity had left me exhausted, both physical and mentally. I could not possibly return to the school because of the noise, the risk of infection from the students and I'd feel under scrutiny every time I went out of the room. It was important that I convalesced in a more suitable environment.

I was still receiving my sick pay from the school, so Marisa and I rented a one bedroom flat in Bishop's Stortford. Our place was the top part of a house in Apton Road, and was very big in comparison to our room on the ward. The entrance from the front garden led up a narrow steep flight of stairs to the first floor where there was a kitchen, a bathroom and a dining room. The bedroom was up more steep stairs in the attic.

The day of our discharge came and the relief we felt was indescribable. Our optimism was more guarded this time due to our recent poor record. All the nurses joked that I had broken the record for days spent on the ward. My goal was to now put several trouble free weeks together out of hospital. Then I knew I had a real chance of improving.

16

MY WORST NIGHTMARE

It was great to be out but unfortunately it did not last. The problem occurred on the morning of 19 November when I awoke barely able to breathe with a severe pain in the right side of my groin. We had been out of Barts for only ten days when the pain struck with terrifying ferocity. It seemed we had just unpacked our bags in the apartment when the pain struck. Biting back the fear and anger, I ignored it but as before, it gradually wore me down. We rang Madge and she contacted Barts who arranged for an ambulance to fetch me because I was immobilised with the pain, and had no hope of getting down the steep stairs. My local GP came and gave me a pain-killing injection but it had little effect.

The ambulance crew arrived and immediately realised that the design of the house rendered a stretcher useless because the top landing was too narrow. They had no option but to secure me into a chair taken from the ambulance and carry me down the stairs. I was in agony with my groin and had to keep my leg stretched straight out in front of me. They picked me up and set off down the perilous descent.

'I feel like Eddie the Eagle or a downhill skier,' I

exclaimed as I peered down the twenty-four steps. 'I could almost bungee jump from here.'

The two ambulance men laughed and continued slowly downwards. Sweat beads surfaced on their necks and they were both sucking in air under the strain.

'Well-done lads,' I ventured meekly, but I was only greeted by grunts of thanks. Eventually we touched down, much to everyone's relief. The ambulance crew was exhausted but had little time to recuperate because I was suffering terribly and they had to get me through the heavy London traffic to the hospital.

It was the same old story. Out and in and out and in. Boomerang Byrne they called me. I was distraught at the thought of going back but I had no choice in the matter. The pain in my groin was dreadful and I was immediately subjected to dozens of drugs, drips and injections. Once more 'The Team' took plenty of blood cultures in an attempt to identify what was wrong. They discovered that the source of the pain was from an infection in my right hip, and on 23 November they decided to open the area and clean the whole joint.

When I awoke I was back on the ward but in a room on my own. My right leg was bandaged from waist to toe and was very painful and irritatingly itchy with all the wrapping on it. Any remote aspirations I had had of ever running competitively again ended that day. An unknown junior doctor casually informed me that I had had a major hip operation and that the area would be sore for up to a year.

'We will send a physiotherapist this afternoon because it's imperative that you immediately move your hip and toes. We don't want you developing a limp now do we?'

'But what about my running?'

'Running? Listen, if you recover so that you can walk properly, then that will be an achievement. I would not even dream about running again. That joint will be too weak to take the pounding on a road or track.'

I was devastated. I wanted to scream and yell. Instead I just cried. It finally all got to me now that my running had been taken from me. My worst nightmare come true.

Later that night, when Marisa was having a bath down the corridor, I managed to sit up in the bed after a fierce struggle. My black diary stared at me invitingly, so I took it and attempted to pen my thoughts. The task proved beyond me and in a violent rage I flung it across the room in disgust.

Letters in my head conceived on doses of morphine, cyclazine and pain. Dictaphone recordings.

TO THE ONE ABOVE: 27-11-94

I, as you know, am not too good. Whatever dignity I had has surely now been swept away with the events of the past few days. Until recently I felt that I had undergone my fair share of humiliation. But last week! First off I had to have my testicles and willy Ultra-sounded which is a strange experience at the best of times. Some men might not complain about having gel rubbed all over them while they lie back and enjoy it. However, as usual in my circumstances, the task was performed by two women and the one doing the gelling and the moving of body parts was very pretty indeed. Now this hip operation which, apart from being extremely painful, has destroyed my running career and also left me somewhat incapacitated. So, the burning question is why did I get diarrhoea? Talk about timing. The problem is that I feel terrible for Marisa. Nobody could feel anything but humble after what she has been through. I have thrown up more times than I care to remember and I've been groped, examined from head to toe, X-rayed, scanned and pictured all ends up but now this. The Big D. Plastered from hip to toe, weak and vulnerable, I am in no position to execute the lightning speed and skill required to reach the toilet in time. Marisa helped me to get some if not all of it into a basin and then of course organise the clean-up operation afterwards. I feel so angry, humiliated, and helpless. Please help. Yours in anticipation of constipation. Mark

The effects of the drugs meant that I had very poor levels of memory, concentration and hand eye coordination. Being near me with a cup of tea in my hand is as dangerous as getting into the ring with Mike Tyson. Only yesterday, when John and Norah were here, did it become apparent just how bad my control was. I attempted to sign some bank forms and John had serious doubts whether they would accept my signature. My writing was like the meandering of a drunken spider, a description once used by a fellow teacher after reading my end of year reports. It is strange, because when I know I cannot do something, then I get a strong urge to do it. Right now my head is full of letters. I want to write to all sorts of people, so I am going to record my thoughts.

To Mam and Dad, 30 November 1994.

My hip is very sore. The pain in my hip was caused by an infection, Septic Arthritis, which may be due to all the chemo, steroids and radiotherapy. Margarita is here from and sends her love. You both are a huge inspiration to me. Maybe I'll see you all at Christmas. Happy birthday Mam.

Whenever Madge and Michele arrived, it was a real jolt to the quiet surrounds of the ward and helped break the monotonous routine of life in a hospital. They usually came straight from work to visit and to keep us informed of the latest gossip from the school. Even when I was too tired to talk, Marisa enjoyed having company and someone to talk to.

'So 'Hop Along' is awake. Feeling better?' asked Michele.

'Dreaming about the summer months. It seems such a long time ago, yet the reality is that I am still here.'

'Don't worry,' added Madge, 'we've brought you more Christmas cards from the kids at school.'

As it was, the room was completely covered in cards of all shapes and sizes. Combined with different posters and decorations, our room was the most colourful and interesting one on the ward. We regularly received comments from the medical staff and workers who entered our room and who were impressed by its décor.

'How are you finding the crutches?' Madge asked.

'Hard work because I do not have the strength in my shoulders to bear the weight.'

'You're a real mess, Mr Byrne,' she added.

'And he's bald,' joked Michele.

'The hardest part is trying to walk between the rails without holding on to anything. It's tough because I know I'm walking with a limp yet it's so difficult to walk correctly because it hurts.'

Marisa arrived back with the teas and biscuits.

'Hello honey, how are you?'

'I'm alright, but I got a terrible fright seeing these two eejits walking in on me.'

'Thank God,' added Madge 'I'm gumming for a cuppa. It's the only reason we come.'

'That and to see if Casualty and ER are doing it right,' piped in Michele.

'Do you want to see the scar?'

'Is that where the stitches were?' said Madge, leaning over the bed to have a look at my hip.

'Stitches,' I roared in protest. 'Iron rods more like it. Here, look at what I wrote in my diary.'

Diary: 2 December 1994. Bodley Scottt 3 Barts.

The cast is now off my hip. It is very ugly and displays all the colours of a rainbow. Elaine cut out the iron staples from my hip with a pliers type instrument. I saw the huge gorge of a cut. The whole area is numb and extremely painful and I felt like a rose bush being pruned in the spring. I have to try and walk up and down three steps, which is incredibly difficult and painful. It is so hard to walk without a limp but I will manage it.

'The physiotherapist told him that it will take a long time before he will walk properly again but that he is making good progress. She said that the muscles around his hip might be numb for up to a year or even longer,' said Marisa.

'It's good that you're so used to pushing yourself as an athlete,' said Michele. 'Mentally and physically you are so much stronger than the average person but Sebastian Coe's record is safe because by the time you get out you'll be with the over sixties.'

'But will I ever pass a drugs test after all this? We counted sixty tablets the other day. Sixty tablets. No wonder I feel sick.'

To Brian, Elizabeth & Family. Pocatello Idaho, 7-12-94

It's hard to believe it but this summer will be ten years since I went to America. Life has really changed since my days in Pocatello. You would not recognise my shattered body. I am bald and weigh about 115 pounds. My stomach and face are bloated from the steroids and I look like a psycho. I long to be back running with an ache that burns within me. The pain I feel in missing it hurts almost as much as the pain in my hip. Luckily I have the experiences of my athletics to help me pull through the cancer. It is definitely helping me recover because I am mentally very tough, having trained and raced for so many years. Although I am physically weaker than I could ever have imagined, my strength lies in my head. Positive thoughts and attitude were as vital then in competition as they are now in my battle to get better. It is good to focus on the positive points. I imagine my body working to overcome the infections and diseases that are within me. It is the same as when I would visualise before a race about how I was going to run and what kind of power I would feel crossing the finish line, the winner.

I am finally beginning to move around better now. The marks of the staples and the bruising from my recent hip operation look as if a graffiti artist has just done a Bronx special on me. The physiotherapy department measured me for a walking stick. I feel so impatient, even though I know it's going to take months, if not a year, to recover from this. My appearance at the Olympics will have to be put on hold for a while. The flat we rented is totally unsuitable because of my hip operation. Immediately inside our front door I have to get up fourteen steps, and then from the landing up to the bedroom there are sixteen even steeper ones. Say Happy Christmas to everyone. MARK

We were released on 9 December. I was supplied with crutches, a walking stick and a bag load of tablets. I could really feel the wintry weather and the change from the ward, where it was always hot. All around us people were preparing for Christmas and it was very exciting sampling the atmosphere. I tried to move my hip as much as possible but it always hurt and secretly I worried if I would ever walk, let alone run again?

John and Norah came over after our release and one day they went shopping with Marisa for a Christmas tree and some decorations. I did not go as I knew that Stortford would be busy; the pain in my hip was making me very sluggish and tired. On their return they set about decorating the place. For a few hours life was perfect. The apartment looked great and everyone was happy.

Slowly however, I got a terrible sick feeling in my stomach. The alarm bells started going off inside my body once again. Instantly I knew what was happening and it saddened me. I hoped against hope that I was being paranoid and imaging the whole thing. However, just like with the initial lump, and all the other setbacks, I could ignore it no longer. I broke the silence.

'I have a pain in my right shoulder.'

'Is it a strong pain?' asked Marisa, the first to react, having heard me say that all too often before.

'Do you have some medication or pain killers?' asked Norah who nursed children in intensive care. They all sprang into action. John helped me sit up. Norah went for the water and Marisa for the drugs. I took two tablets and got out of the bed and moved around to try to keep out of the limelight. It was a futile effort; nothing improved and with a heavy heart I made a phone call.

'Hello, an incredibly bewildered woman speaking,' joked Madge as she answered the phone.

'Hi Madge, I'm afraid I need to go back to the Barts.'

'I'll be over in a minute, darling.'

My mind was swimming somewhere between 'Apocalypse Now' and 'Papillon'. I was confused, angry and bitter. I was so tired of all the pain and frustration. Just nine days after being released, I was back on one of those bloody trolleys heading towards the operating theatre. I could hardly remember what it was like to be outside the walls of Barts for any length of time. The pain in my shoulder was matched only by the anguish of disappointment. Then, like vultures on the Serengeti, the masked ones closed in on me and stuck a sharp needle into my vein.

I came to and coughed up some vomit on myself. Then Daniel arrived.

'You cannot stay away,' he began.

'Believe me, I am trying. I think Barts has a huge tractor beam homed in on me. What's wrong this time?'

'It's another joint infection. We didn't grow anything from the cultures yet, but these joint problems are a consequence of all the treatment and drugs you've had. Don't forget I promised to have you out by Christmas, and you do know that I am finishing here next week.'

'Yes, and we are not happy about it,' I replied. 'I find it hard to change doctors when I have a good one like you. The vast majority of the doctors and nurses are tremendous at helping and explaining things but, there are always a few who are either incapable or unwilling to deal on a personal level with patients. Some have prodded and poked me without a please or a thank you and their aloof attitudes can make patients feel very insignificant. Maybe they should swap with a sick person for a day to see how hard it is. Anyway enough of my ranting; you have been great. I never felt that you were in a hurry to get in and out of the room or that you minded spending time to explain everything.'

'Have you heard anything about your job?' he asked.

'No. That's the problem when you're sick. Life goes on regardless, and problems like coping with cancer, worrying about my family, my job, money and everything else still have to be dealt with. All I can do is get better.'

'I am sure that you will. You are a fighter.'

'Thanks,' I said. 'Thanks for everything.'

Dictaphone 21 December 1994. To Brent in Idaho.

Lying in a hospital bed, as I have been now for such a long time, just reinforces the comments that we never fully appreciate life when we are healthy. Whenever I start to feel sorry for myself I look out of my window to see the children's hospital and the little kids with various cancers and it soon focuses my mind. The year is nearly over and I have survived my Annus Horribilis. I hope I never have to face a year like that again. I must look forward now and be positive. Keep well and take care. Roll on 1995.

At ten in the morning on Christmas Eve, we were finally allowed to leave the hospital. I had won the bet, but only just.

'Well, Mr Byrne, you cut it pretty fine,' Professor Lister began. 'We will, of course, have to see you in three days for a check up. Debbie or Susan will make the appointments for you. Have a great Christmas.'

'The same to you. Thanks once again.'

Madge picked us up later in the day and brought us to our flat. It was a vibrant happy place as Mam and Dad had come from Ireland, Margarita from Spain and together with Ian, Catherine and Madge, we celebrated in style. Margarita transported half of Andalucía with her, including prawns, chorizos, tortilla, wine, olives, and croquetas. It was an amazing spread and my only regret was that I could eat so little of it; however, the real reward was being out of the hospital and reunited with loved ones.

On New Year's Eve we all gathered again in our flat and were joined by our neighbours Anne and Aidan Leacy and their family, James, Aidan and Anne, Madeleine, Peter, Dominic and Jane. It was a truly moving and festive time. We celebrated the passing of a dreadful year and looked forward with hope to a better, brighter one. Toasts were made, songs sung and people kissed with reckless abandon.

PART THREE

17

THE ROAD TO HELL

I realised from the start of my illness that I had to be positive and determined. I did not want to let the cancer control me and to become angry and bitter with everyone and everything. That would have been a totally negative and destructive response. I did not want to live every day regretting the fact that my running career had been cut short in its prime.

Initially when I became ill, I kept telling myself that I would get back to running and my old life again, but as time passed by, reality dawned and I knew that I would never be able to compete again on a running track. However, I was determined to follow in the footsteps of countless others who overcame far greater difficulties than I had experienced. I wanted to rebuild my life and I knew that by being positive, happy and outgoing I had the chance to achieve just that.

Life out of Barts was exquisite. Our place was a most welcome change to the ward. At first I returned to Barts twice a week for blood and platelet transfusions. The umbilical cord was starting to stretch a little bit. The threat of a setback was ever present but every morning when I awoke my immediate feeling was one of relief and gratitude to be alive. I struggled every day to cope with the pain and tiredness, but it was a small price to pay for being out of hospital. My rehabilitation was a very monotonous, painful process which required self-discipline to perform the daily strength and flexibility exercises. My hip and shoulder needed constant work but I did this on my own at home rather than going all the way in to Barts. However, it was more satisfying doing it myself because I was in control of the situation and taking positive steps to recover my health.

Exercising again reminded me of the times that I used to run around the fields at the club in Blackrock. We ran in all conditions and loved it. I remembered the pain that I would get near the end of a hard session or a race when lactic acid built up in my muscles. How I would will myself on to the finish determined to get there. Every stride and breath I took burned deep into my lungs and chest as my muscles slowly seized up, yet I would fight and push myself to the limit.

I soon progressed from the crutches to a walking stick which the physiotherapy department made for me. Descending and negotiating the steep stairs of the flat was a perilous task, yet it did help to build my hip muscles. Apton Road was on a hill leading down into the town, so at first I walked down to the public car park, which was about two hundred yards away. Because of the steep hill, the walk back was very hard and, once I was back in the flat, I was a spent force for the rest of the day.

I looked forward to the time when I would be physically fitter and not so drug-dependent. My current list of daily tablets included ones for anti-shingles, tuberculosis, antibiotics, anti-ulcer, painkillers, plus anti-sickness. Each day posed a new challenge but everyone was delighted that I was out of the hospital again. I was just happy to be alive. It was now a case of 'carpe diem' which means 'seize the day'. I was determined not to become paranoid and withdrawn, thinking about every pain and the possibility of a setback. Instead Marisa and I made it our priority to enjoy and cherish every minute of every day.

The week of John and Norah's wedding I suffered a traumatic upset. Any hope that I had harboured of attending vanished as quickly as the pain that appeared in my left shoulder. On 13 March we packed our bags, phoned Madge and Barts. By the time we got there I was in considerable distress and was admitted immediately onto the ward. My shoulder completely locked up and I could not bear anyone to touch it. Despite my obvious anguish, I had an argument with an insensitive and rude doctor who wanted to take my blood pressure. I was incensed at the cheek of a medic arguing like that with a sick person in such obvious pain. I spent a dreadful night on the ward where I received the usual transfusions of blood and platelets. Once more I was whisked off to the theatre for an operation to remove pus from my joint.

The words 'septic and reactive arthritis' were used by 'The Team' when they came to explain what had happened. I was hospitalised for another three weeks. Recuperation was slow and each passing day increased my anxiety about going to Ireland to see my Dad. There was no doubt that he was suffering more and I was desperate to go home to be with him. One or two problems had really knocked him back and as time dragged by, my worry increased. My heart longed to see, and to spend time with, my Dad and Mam, and as more reports came of Dad's struggle and weakness, my desire grew stronger by the hour.

My biggest problem, apart from the pain in my joints, was my platelet count. They never recovered from the transplant and were still well below normal, which made it too dangerous for me to fly. Flying in a pressurised cabin together with the effects of the take off and descent, might lead to internal bleeding which could cause serious problems. Since I had already experienced the pain of an internal bleed in my ear and subsequent deafness, I could not take the risk. I worried that something would happen to Dad while I was trapped in England and my parents were unable to visit me. My ultimate fear was that I would never see him again. The 21 June was to be his 69th birthday and I hoped to make it for his party.

John and Norah's wedding came and went without us being able to attend, but after their honeymoon, they came to England to stay with us for a while. My Dad had thankfully made it through the day but by all accounts he was now very thin and weak and suffering from other complications. His main discomfort was a terrible itch all over his body and a constant sickness in his stomach owing to bile in his system, which also turned his skin to a yellow complexion.

At the end of March I heard that my marriage was annulled, even though now that seemed completely unimportant and almost a different life after all that had happened in the few years since then. It was worlds apart because my life had changed so spectacularly. Indeed, I as an individual had changed so much in eight years.

Throughout May I enjoyed quite a good spell and Marisa and I were happily settled into the flat. However, two weeks after celebrating the first anniversary of my bone marrow transplant, I returned yet again to Barts on 31 May with a terrible pain in my right shoulder. The excruciating pain locked my shoulder and they took me off to operate on it.

My mood was sullen, as I had not planned for so many post transplant problems. I really believed that a year after the transplant I would be much better. Exasperated and on the verge of imploding, my confidence was being tested to breaking point. My joint operations now stood at four: right hip once, right shoulder twice and left shoulder once. This time I had a tube protruding from my arm as a drain and a decent-sized scar to match. I was hospitalised for nine days in a ward with five others and I encountered the normal sleepless nights, snoring, groans and noises which were an unwelcome déjà vu. Marisa could not sleep on a mattress since the other patients might fall over her, so she found a reclining chair, pulled it up beside my bed and closed the curtains around us.

We had now lived in Barts for ninety per cent of the past year. I knew every building and recognised every sound and smell on the ward. If I had had shares in the place, I would have been a millionaire. I was sick of the sight of needles, nurses, doctors, and being in pain. I wanted out, and soon. I was seriously beginning to doubt how long I could keep dealing with the cacophony of events and the multitude of problems. Every drug, needle, operation and ordeal affected me both physically and mentally, weakening my ailing body little by little.

On release from Barts I was allowed to stop taking the anti-shingles tablets which I had been on for a whole year. I felt that at least was one milestone; no more Zovirax tablets which meant five less tablets a day. Marisa turned the flat into a comfortable, pleasant place to live and each day passed quietly. I performed my shoulder exercises religiously and a week after being let out I talked to Mam and Dad about coming home.

'Don't worry if you can't come,' Dad said, 'just keep getting stronger. I'm fine and there will be plenty more birthdays.'

I really wanted to go but, unfortunately, my joint problems prevented me from travelling. Dad's birthday party was a great success on a glorious summer's day and we agreed to have a joint party in July for Mam and Dad's fortieth wedding anniversary and my thirty-first birthday.

25 June arrived and with it a nasty pain in my left eye. It had persisted for some days and by Saturday night the pain had intensified to such a degree that I returned to Barts in a terrible state. A junior doctor, who I did not know, came to examine me in one of the rooms.

'Oh that's shingles,' he said flippantly and far too casually for my liking.

'It can't be shingles. I just stopped the Acyclovir tablets after a whole bloody year.'

'You stopped too early then, but we can treat it,' he snapped.

'I was told to stop,' I fumed angrily. 'I took five tablets every single day without fail for a whole year and practically lived here for months on end. Now just three weeks after stopping them, I have got shingles. That's disgusting. I won't believe it.'

'Your immune system is still weak,' he stammered.

'Tell me about it,' I spat sarcastically. 'I don't know if it will ever be normal again.'

He left to get someone else to look at me and to make arrangements for a bed. I was angry and shocked.

'How could I get shingles?' I pleaded to Marisa.

'I'm sorry, love; it's really unfair.'

We sat in silence whilst I waited for news of a bed. Jonathan Shamash, who had recently become my latest doctor at Barts, arrived later.

'Let's have a look at your head and eye.'

'I really can't believe this is happening. I only stopped a few weeks ago. Are you sure it's shingles?'

'Definitely. You will probably have to stay in for three weeks, but I have to warn you that the pain can last for several months. We will get you into a room and start the Acyclovir through a drip.'

'Great, more cannulae. Is this ever going to end?'

Later we were shown to a side room because, with shingles, I had to be isolated, which at least spared us the horrors of the ward. It also meant that Marisa could stay in the room, which she did, even though shingles were highly contagious and she might catch them. I was devastated. Alone, the tears swelled quickly and burst forward. Marisa consoled me but all I could think of was betrayal.

I was, after all, back in hospital yet again. Elaine arrived with 'Drippy' and I was flooded intravenously with Acyclovir so that I could receive larger quantities of it. I found the constant pain in my eye extremely hard to cope with. Isolated and unable to move out of the room I was haggard and worn out. The constant battle with pain, distress and multiple difficulties left me emaciated and desperately tired.

Several times a day I had cream put on the sores and drops put in my eyes, which were uncomfortable experiences. Hours passed and, like a prisoner, I was shackled to 'Drippy'. I resented having to drag that damn thing everywhere I went. In anger I kicked it brutally but still it clung to me like a faithful hound.

Three days later Jonathan came to see me. He told me that because of all of my setbacks over the past several months that they were going to start me on some new injections called Eprex Epoetin. They would inject me three times a week and he was convinced that the Eprex would definitely help.

'Don't be so sure,' I said a little sceptically. 'Jokes about being a garden sprinkler are no longer funny.'

Marisa cleansed my eyes regularly. I attended the eye clinic twice a week to ensure that my eyesight was not damaged. It was an uncomfortable process since I had to put my eye up against a weird kind of contraption for a doctor to shine a bright light into it. This enabled them to examine my eye and administer the drops and creams. Shingles, or Herpes Zoster, is the same virus that causes childhood chicken pox and can be a really nasty infection. Slowly, as the days passed, the scabs from the shingles crustated and faded.

I received a lot of attention which, whilst it was frustrating, was also vital. I had no intentions of adding blindness to my ever-growing list of ailments which now stood at cancer, septicaemia, deafness of one ear, blood clots, one hip and three shoulder operations, a low blood count, septic arthritis, no platelets, fevers, rashes and, finally, shingles. Predictably, the days on the ward were incredibly dull and tedious because of our familiarity with Barts and I found sleep very hard to come by.

Eventually, after an exhausting three weeks in the hospital, I was released. The shingles had taken a lot out of me and, despite my obvious delight to get out, I did not feel at all well. Like an old ship, battered by a storm, I barely made it home.

The bright hot sunny days badly affected my eye, which, despite having the curtains closed throughout the day, continued to be a source of real irritation. I felt at the nadir of health and emotion. Mentally I was deflated and the combination of pain and fatigue plummeted me back to the days of the Septicaemia when everything was impossible.

I was fed up with the whole situation: the pain in my eye, my lack of platelets and the fact that a year after the transplant my counts were still as poor as ever. I injected myself with the Eprex and prayed that soon it would boost my ailing blood count. The painkillers made me tired, groggy, irritable and unstable on my feet, yet the pain never relinquished its vice-like hold on me.

After two dreadful weeks of being house-bound, we went for a short walk to St Joseph's Church. I walked like a drunk, stumbling and swaying badly. Had it not been for Marisa's support, I would have not have made it. It was a stiflingly hot, humid day and, within five minutes of leaving the house, I threw up on the grassy verge. We sat down for a little rest outside the church and we were half-way back to the house when disaster struck.

My stomach heaved violently and, stumbling to be sick, I keeled over onto the grass. Round and round my head spun and the world with it. I could hear Marisa's voice but I could not see her. Panic and fear gripped me as I tried unsuccessfully to get up. Everything was swimming round and round. I lay on my side, eyes closed, and continued to vomit, not knowing or caring where it went. Later after a tremendous effort I made it to my feet.

'I'll go to the Leacys for James or Aidan,' Marisa told me.

'No don't leave me; I'll be OK. We can make it.'

Our flat was only two hundred yards away but it seemed miles. A wall ran along the footpath; between it and Marisa I advanced towards home. Each step sent a bolting pain shooting throughout my body. My movements were slow, unsteady; my eye, my head and my joints burned in anguish. Several people walked past us but no one stopped to help, assuming that I was a drug addict or that I was drunk. We made it to our garden steps and Marisa went next door and returned with Aidan to help me up the stairs to the bathroom.

'Leave me here,' I gasped and then I threw up again.

I lay there with my head propped against the cold toilet bowl. A new low had been reached, in what seemed a bottomless pit of setbacks and strife. The pain had not abated at all, yet the drugs affected me to a terrifying degree. My voice was badly slurred; my eyesight was hugely impaired and my stomach sick. I felt a broken man.

In a rage I flung all the painkillers in the bin and resorted to using ice packs on my eye. The apartment was not designed to cope with the oppressive heat and so I spent most of the mornings and afternoons lying on a mattress in my boxer shorts, with the curtains drawn. Even though the scars around my eye had disappeared weeks earlier, the sunlight aggravated the pain; I was still mentally and physically shattered and I seriously wondered if the transplant had worked at all.

News from Ireland was not so good. Dad's health had deteriorated further and with that my worries of never seeing him again increased. One day in August John rang.

'How are you feeling now?' he asked.

'Pretty down. I've still got the pain in my eye but the scars are gone and I'm stabbing myself regularly with the Eprex injections. Margarita arrived from Spain today so that's good. How is everyone there?'

'Not bad. Dad's doctor came up today and wants him to go into hospital next Friday for a little operation.'

'What kind of operation?'

'He wants to put a small tube in to relieve some bile, which is making Dad sick and itchy. Dad should only be in hospital for a day or two.'

'I suppose it's a general anaesthetic. Do you think he is strong enough for that?'

'Well he is very weak and I just don't know.'

'My shingles have cleared and I was hoping to come home once the pain in my eye got better, but I don't really like the thought of Dad going into hospital before I see him. Leave it with me and I'll get back to you shortly.'

Instantly I was afraid that he might not come through it. I wanted to see my Dad before he had any operation. My own experience had taught me what a general anaesthetic was like and I was afraid it would be too much for someone in his condition. I rang Ruth and talked to her. Marisa and Margarita, who was a nurse, agreed that we should go to Ireland. Our neighbour, Anne Leacy, offered to take us to Holyhead to get the boat to Dun Laoghaire. Her sister Claire lived in

Cheltenham, which is about two hours from Holyhead, so she could stay there with her. I telephoned Mam and Dad to tell them we were coming and I got a letter from Dr. Shamash for Saint James's Hospital in Dublin in case anything happened to me whilst I was at home.

Two days later, on a scorching hot day, we set off for Holyhead. The journey was an extremely difficult one for me because I suffered the whole way with pains in my eye. We stopped several times to give me a break and finally, some seven hours later, we arrived at the boat. The new catamaran took only ninety minutes to make the crossing to Dun Laoghaire. Ruth met us and drove us to Roundwood.

Mam and Dad were thrilled to see us. My mother looked tired and drawn. My Dad was a picture, sitting in the conservatory looking out at the lake. He was very thin and weak and it was a very emotional homecoming. I almost had to pinch myself that I was finally home after everything had contrived against me. The next day was a beautiful, sunny day. Mam, Ruth, Dermot, John, Norah, Margarita, Marisa and I sat in the garden talking. Dad, who had remained indoors as the weather was too hot for him, suddenly came out to the garden carrying a cassette player.

'I thought the ladies might like to hear this.'

I saw a smile creep across his face as the music began. It was one of John's South American tapes and instantly Margarita and Marisa recognised the tune and they sang along to it. Then, to everyone's amazement, Dad asked Marisa to dance. They gently moved around the lawn adjacent to the fish pond. We sat and clapped them.

It was a poignant moment and one that I will always remember because it completely summed up my father. Even to the end he defied his illness and walked out to the back garden to bring happiness to others. He was a thin, quiet, polite man, yet anyone who met him instantly recognised his natural, sincere manner and goodness. His kindness and sense of humour never left him. He emanated strength, courage, humour and compassion. That summer's day I realised what a great influence he had been in my life and how much I loved him.

My father died in the early hours of the morning of 14 August 1995 in St James's Hospital, Dublin, just three days after his little dance in the garden with Marisa. For three days and three nights the whole family took turns to keep vigil in the hospital, after his operation, as his strength never returned. The night he died, Marisa and I were sleeping in the hospital, so that I could meet the doctors at eight in the morning and get more Eprex injections. I'll always remember the moment the nurse came to our room and turned the light on. Instantly I knew what she was about to say. Mam, Ruth and John had left for home only hours earlier and I had to telephone them with the news.

Dad's battle was over and with it a huge part of all our lives. His funeral was held in Roundwood on a scorching hot summer day. My mother always said that Dad was born in a heat wave, they were married in a heat wave, and now he had passed away in one. There was a tremendous turnout for him and many people commented that it was the nicest funeral they had ever been to. The local Roundwood choir sang his favourite hymns, the church looked lovely and Father John, Dermot's brother, said the mass along with three other priests and a Monsignor.

My Dad never gave up; he was a fighter to the end. It was natural, therefore, that he was my greatest role model. His simple message was to make the most of every day, be happy as often as possible and regularly to stop and to thank God to be still alive. It was also another reminder to me just how close I had come to dying just ten months earlier, and how very lucky I was to be still alive.

18

DON'T LOOK BACK IN ANGER

Three weeks after my father died, we returned to Bishop's Stortford. The next few weeks passed without any major incident, but I thought about him every day. He was there watching over and guiding me. His departure was an enormous loss for us all, especially for my mother. It was a heart-breaking wrench for her after forty happy years together.

Our routine back in England was boring and mundane, yet, for me, it was bliss. I attended Barts regularly and continued with the injections. Jonathan Shamash was still my doctor at Barts and I found the consistency a welcome change.

October 5 1995 made it a year for Marisa's promise. She had not worn any jewellery or had her hair cut for the past year and now she had fulfilled that pledge. It reminded me yet again what a great person she was. A real soul mate.

Christmas came and with it the reality that it was the first one without Dad. A huge hole existed in all our lives without him, especially my mother's, but we consoled ourselves with the knowledge that he was happy up above and looking after us all the time.

The following March I returned to Roundwood to see everyone, but while I was there my shoulder problems flared up again and I was rushed off to St James's Hospital. They operated on my left shoulder for the same infection problems as before. This evened up the count of two operations on each side. As usual, the hospital provided the setting for both sad and funny moments. St James's was, of course, the hospital where my father had died and naturally it was difficult for all of us, especially my Mum, to be back there again.

Recovering that night from my operation, I was woken by singing and loud voices. A man, completely inebriated, had just been put in the bed opposite mine, and he proceeded to give the whole ward a rendition of several songs. A nurse chastised him and tried to get some information out of him. Between insisting that he was Bill Clinton, the President of the United States and bursting into song, he would fart incredibly loudly, and return to blame the rain and not the fifteen pints of Guinness that made him fall and break his leg.

The next day I was moved to a single room because of my immune system and medical history. Unfortunately I started getting dreadful bouts of muscular cramps and had to pack heat pads over my legs to alleviate the pain.

After ten days in hospital, having suffered a great deal with the cramps, I was released with the news that my platelet count was high enough to allow me to fly again. I almost cried for joy when several weeks later Jonathan informed me that my platelets were high enough and I could now stop the injections. And so, almost two years after the transplant, my platelet count had finally risen sufficiently so as not to be such a worry for me.

My joint and cramp problems persisted, but slowly I began to look and feel better. I could walk further each day and my appetite and taste buds were fully restored. Life was all about living in the now, and Marisa, my mother and I went to Spain that September to stay with Margarita for a holiday on the Costa del Sol.

In April 1997, I went with Marisa to Lourdes for Easter and bathed twice in the baths. It was almost exactly three years since we had entered St Bartholomew's for the transplant.

When I was first diagnosed with Non–Hodgkin's Lymphoma, I had absolutely no idea what it was. On my journey of discovery, a whole new world had opened up to me, a vast network of cancer patient organisations working extremely hard to bring information, compassion and understanding to people in need. Some of these, like the Lymphoma Association, BACUP and Cancer Research, help people to realise that they are not alone; that help and advice is available. I used every available outlet to gain insight and information on my illness. I joined the (HDLA), now known as the Lymphoma Association, and I have volunteered to give support and advice from my own experiences to people who are now in a similar situation.

I started to seriously write this book in 1997. A writer requires many of the same disciplines that an athlete needs. Dedication, perseverance, belief in one's ability and that never give up mentality when things are not going well. It can be a lonely frustrating job and for this book reliving some of the past years has at times been an emotionally tough journey to travel. However, despite that, I am thrilled that it has finally come to fruition.

In 1998 Marisa and I won a Valentine's weekend trip to New York. It was a great surprise and a brilliant present after the stress of the previous years. We met up with a hundred other lucky couples in 'The Love Lounge' and we really had an amazing time.

Now our routine is back to normal. If my bones are sore I take it easy and try to write, if they are okay I enjoy the garden and a nice walk. Generally we live a very quite calm life in Bishop's Stortford. Some people might find it boring and wonder how we can be with each other twenty-four hours a day seven days a week, but after all that has happened, we have found a certain peace and contentment in our lives. We love watching movies and if nothing is on, then I'll go and listen to some music, on vinyl of course.

Madge, Catherine and Ian live close by and we see them three or four times a week. Michele has just moved jobs but we keep in touch and see her about once a month. Sandra and Ciarán, Barbara and Caroline, the Leacys and all our other friends in and around Bishop's Stortford are well and getting on with life. The lads at home are still a very important part of my life and I love going back to Ireland to meet up with them for a few pints. I am so lucky to have them as we go back a long way, back to when we were together in primary and secondary school.

January 2000 made it seven years since I was diagnosed with cancer and six years for my sister Ruth. Ruth had a scare when she discovered another lump two years ago but in true determined style she overcame that setback and battled back. She has a very strong constitution and a positive outlook. She has check-ups every few months now and is enjoying a happy and full life with Dermot. My nieces Aisling and Tara have just left school while Simon is already in secondary school.

John and Norah, who had just moved to Paris, announced the birth of their second child, Liam Mark. Their first baby, Seán, was born within days of John's birthday and Dad's anniversary. John and I still have great banter about Manchester United and Arsenal and regularly discuss all the current sport with passion. My Mum has coped remarkably well and works as hard as ever in the garden which is a great testament to all that Dad and she achieved over the years together. She is a power of strength and amazes me still with her resilience and drive. Every time I see her reminds me how lucky I was to have such great parents. She has now taken up painting and is showing a real talent at it.

Marisa and I moved from our flat to a rented house in another part of Bishop's Stortford. Having the bigger space and our own garden is fantastic and we have started growing vegetables. Marisa is amazingly still putting up with me, and my Spanish has now improved. At last I can talk to Margarita about most things, but especially her passion for Real Madrid. Marisa and I have a great time together. Who knows, we may even live in Spain or Ireland one day.

My visits and association with St Bartholomew's is gradually being stretched to twice a year. I now attend the London Hospital to see Dr. D'Cruz about my joints. Apart from my joint problems and the muscular cramps, which can be very painful, life is good and I am happy to be alive. Every day I have pain of some description, as my joints are sore and troublesome. A recent Infecton Scan showed that I am riddled with reactive and septic arthritis and that that I have Avascular Necrosis. This is where the blood supply cannot get to the bones and they eventually seize up and joint replacements will most likely be necessary. However that is in the future and right now I am mentally and emotionally strong and confident.

Mine is a success story made possible only by an infinite number of people who are too numerous to mention. However, they know who they are. They are my family and friends and the amazing nurses, doctors and staff at St Bartholomew's and the London Hospital. To all who help me to live the fiesta every day I say a huge thank you.

Writing this book has opened up new doors for me. Having tried to emulate the many famous Irish sporting heroes, I am now aspiring to follow in the footsteps of O'Casey, Yeats and Wilde. Already I have caught the bug and I have started on some scripts for a movie. Who knows, next stop Hollywood. This book is in celebration and thanks for all the help and encouragement I have received, and especially in tribute to all who have, in whatever way shape or form, 'kicked the devil in the shins'.

I hope it will inspire anyone who is currently suffering from a problem or illness that may be affecting them to fight back and never give in. Go on; give it a good kick in the shins. You know you can do it.

I believe that I am clear, cured of all cancer. I believe that I will survive and that is how I propose to live for as long as possible. There was a time when going back to my job was one of my goals and something that drove me on to get better; however, as time passed and my problems continued, the school hired new people. As a history teacher, I fully appreciate the past but more often now I prefer to celebrate the present and raise a glass to the future.

Of course it is a sobering experience that I have been through; but that is all the more reason not to think negatively about the horrors of the past or the uncertainties of the future. I regard it as a stage in my life, an experience, something to learn from and to carry with me into the future. Don't look back in anger I hear you say, and thankfully I do not. Live in the now and seize the day like Robin Williams told his pupils in 'Dead Poets Society'.

I did not find the glory I set out for by running and winning the Olympics, but I found glory in surviving and living new experiences. I have met some great characters both on and off the ward, who, with their special brand of humour and outlook on life, have added enormously to that of my own. Live on the edge and 'kick the devil in the shins' each and every single day. There is no doubt that I feel I have emerged a stronger person better equipped to deal with life and any new setbacks that may come my way. Now and then various blood tests, joint or skin problems arise but I strive to deal with them calmly and without too much stress or fuss.

Having gone through terrible pain and suffering, I have thankfully managed to come through with my sense of humour still intact. My appreciation for life has been significantly increased by my experiences. Now I strive to draw from all that has happened to help me be as constructive and as happy as possible. As far as I am concerned, these are the happiest days of my life.

Someone recently asked me if I miss running and I replied that it has never left me. It cannot; it is in my blood, no matter how much chemotherapy or how many transfusions I have had. I did it all my life because I loved it and I will always have the memories of those unique experiences. It was a privilege to have lived that lifestyle. My passion for life has been enhanced, turned up a notch.

A few weeks ago I went back to Blackrock running club with Marisa to see the lads there. They were still charging around the track with dozens of youngsters behind them, living the dream. I received a great welcome.

'You haven't changed.'

'You look younger and in better shape now.'

'Eamonn Coghlan became the first man over forty to run under four minutes for the mile, so there is hope for you yet. What with all those drugs in you, you never know.'

I wonder if I could start training again; but I do not know where my spikes are. I wonder if I could start training again, but I do not know if my shorts still fit. It would be great, all right, to get out there again; maybe Marisa will join me. Over forty, was he? Well I still have my stopwatch and we could go tomorrow...and, yes, maybe I could run. What I need is a plan. I wonder what letter I am at now?

Hey
A runner is a strange man the likes appeals to me
He runs the tough hilly roads, a pacer he could be
All he has is his shoes, his singlet shorts and socks
To beat the hills, the dogs and pills
To beat the bloody lot
The cold can be fierce the wind so strong
He battles hard he battles long
The nights damp the sun long gone
He battles hard and he runs on
The rain can lash wind howl gale force
But he runs on, blisters burst

Round and round a sun baked track,
Burning feet, heaving chest, sweating,
just about to crack
lactic acid, shortening stride, leaning for the finish
leaden legs, muscle tighten in your back
Cross the line, quick check the watch,
barely able to breathe
A stagger, a walk, the task complete
off he goes for more

Some do it in search of fame
Some because they love it
Some run because it's so pure
Some for love and passion

And so a running man is strange
To this every day
I am such a running man
And I am happy and free and hey